SIMPLIFICATION OF CUSTOMS PROCEDURES:
REDUCING TRANSACTION COSTS FOR EFFICIENCY, INTEGRITY, AND TRADE FACILITATION

Edited by
Salvatore Schiavo-Campo

D1670091

Asian Development Bank

November 1999

Contents

Acronyms   v

Foreword   ix
Tadao Chino

Introduction: The Fiscal and Governance Dimension
of Customs Simplification   1
Salvatore Schiavo-Campo

I – RECENT INTERNATIONAL INITIATIVES FOR CUSTOMS SIMPLIFICATION

1. Trade Facilitation Efforts of ASEM and Japan   13
   Hiroshi Arichi
2. The World Customs Organization and Trade
   Facilitation   23
   Rob van Kuik
3. Activities of the Asia-Pacific Economic
   Cooperation Forum   29
   Ibrahim bin Md. Isa

II – IMPROVING SERVICE AND EFFICIENCY IN CUSTOMS

4. The Role of the World Trade Organization   37
   Hans van Bodegraven
5. A Customs System for Improved Service and
   Efficiency   49
   Patrick Heinesson
6. Risk Analysis: A New Tool for Customs
   Efficiency and Enforcement   57
   Rafael Arana

7. The Role of Information Technology in Customs
    Modernization   65
    Buenaventura Maniego
8. Relations Between Customs and Private
    Operators in Finland   73
    Leo Nissinen

III – THE AIRLINE INDUSTRY: A CASE STUDY

9. Customs Simplification: An International Airline
    Perspective   81
    Geoffrey Barrington
10. The Integrated Air Express Industry   89
    James Goh
11. Air Cargo Facilitation   99
    Robert Richardson

Annexes

I   Survey of Customs Reform and Modernization
     Trends and Best Practices   109
     World Customs Organization
II   Compendium of Trade Facilitation
     Recommendations   135
     *United Nations Conference on Trade and
     Development*
III Summary of Efforts by ASEM & Japan Towards   153
     Trade Facilitation
IV   Technical Assistance to Kingdom of Nepal for
     Efficiency Enhancement of Customs Operations:
     An Example of ADB Assistance   161

Note on Contributors   167

Acronyms

ACOS	Automated Customs Operations Systems
ADB	Asian Development Bank
AEBF	Asian-Europe Business Forum
AEM	ASEAN Economic Ministers Meeting
AFTA	ASEAN Free Trade Area
AHTN	ASEAN Harmonization Tariff Nomenclature
APEC	Asia Pacific Economic Cooperation
APEC BMC	APEC Budget and Management Committee
APEC-SCCP	APEC-Sub-Committee on Customs Procedures
APEC TILF	APEC Trade and Investment Liberalization and Facilitation Fund
ASEAN	Association of Southeast Asian Nations
ASEM	Asia-Europe Meeting
ASEM DG-C	ASEM Directors-General and Commissioners Meeting
ASEM TFAP	ASEM Trade Facilitation Action Plan
ASYCUDA	Automated Systems for Customs Data Management
ATI	Asian Terminal Incorporated
BIDA	Brokers and Importers Data Access
BOI	Binding Origin Information
CAPs	collective action plans
CAPEC	Conference of Asia-Pacific Express Carriers
CCBI	Chamber of Customs Brokers, Incorporated
CCMAA	Customs Cooperation and Mutual Administrative Assistance Agreements
CDEC	Consolidators Data Exchange Centre
CDSS	Customs Decision Support System
CIF	cost, insurance, and freight
DMCs	developing member countries
DTI	Direct Traders Input facility

EC	European Commission
EDI	electronic data interchange
EMM	Economic Ministers Meeting
EU	European Union
FOB	free-on-board
GATT	General Agreement on Tariffs and Trade
G7	Group of Seven
HCV	Harmonization of Customs Valuation
HS	Harmonized System
IAPs	individual action plans
IATA	International Air Transport Association
IECC	International Express Carriers Conference
IEG	Investment Experts Group
IMF	International Monetary Fund
IPAP	Investment Promotion Action Plan
IT	information technology
MDBs	multilateral development banks
MOU	memorandum of understanding
NACCS	Nippon Automated Cargo Clearance System
NAFTA	North American Free Trade Agreement
OECD	Organization of Economic Cooperation and Development
PCCI	Philippine Chamber of Commerce and Industry
PFI	Philippine Federation of Industries
PTCP	Philippine Tax Computerization Program
PUC	Philippine Users Confederation
RILO	Regional Intelligence Liaison Offices
SAD	single administrative document
SEOM	Senior Economic Officials Meeting
SITA	Société Internationale de Télecommunications Aéronautiques
SOMTI	Senior Officials Meeting on Trade and Investment
SPS	Sanitary and Phytosanitary Procedures

TCRO	Technical Committee on Rules of Origin
UN	United Nations
UN CEFACT	UN Centre for the Facilitation of Procedures and Practices for Administration, Commerce and Transport
UNDP	UN Development Programme
UNCTAD	UN Conference on Trade and Development
UR	Uruguay Round
WB	World Bank
WCO	World Customs Organization
WTO	World Trade Organization
WTO-TRIPS	WTO-Intellectual Property Rights Agreement

Foreword

It was a great pleasure for us at the Asian Development Bank to host the Asia-Europe Meeting (ASEM) Seminar on Harmonization and Simplification of Customs Procedures, held on 23–26 February 1999, in cooperation with the Philippine Bureau of Customs and the private sector. It was unusual and noteworthy to assemble in a single venue high-level officials and private-sector leaders from the 15 member countries of the European Union (EU) and 10 Asian countries, both developed and developing, as well as representatives of major international organizations such as the EU itself, the Association of Southeast Asian Nations (ASEAN), and the World Customs Organization (WCO).

The ADB is the premier regional development bank for Asia and the Pacific, working independently but in partnership with the World Bank, the European Commission (EC), ASEAN, and other multilateral and bilateral organizations. The Bank is owned by 57 countries, of which 41 are from the region; the others include many of the European countries represented at the ASEM. In recent years, Bank assistance to developing member countries has averaged over US$7 billion a year. This includes an annual grant assistance of over US$150 million, of which a significant proportion is provided through the Japan Special Fund. The Japanese Special Fund also contributed significant resources which have made the ASEM seminar possible.

ADB has been transforming itself from a project lender into a broad-based development institution to meet the changing and increasingly complex needs of the developing member countries, with poverty reduction as the overarching goal. This transformation calls for even closer cooperation with a variety of other international efforts. This is one reason why we welcomed the opportunity to support and host this seminar. There is another important reason. The Bank is vitally concerned with issues of governance and corruption, because good governance is indispensable for sound economic management and sustained development, and corruption is very costly, particularly for the poor. Customs procedures and processes are at the heart of these issues. I am confident that the papers presented in this book will make a good contribution to the analysis and the dialogue, as well and set a key precedent for continuing similar collaborative efforts in the future, in order to make tangible progress toward procedural streamlining, in the common interest of all concerned.

Tadao Chino
President
Asian Development Bank

Introduction
The Economic and Governance Dimensions of Customs Procedures*

Salvatore Schiavo-Campo

T his introduction is aimed at providing a broad context to the apparently technical questions of procedural simplification in customs. Much of the following is familiar material, but necessary to underline the important linkages between the customs function and the overall economic system. The subject of customs procedures appears technical, narrow, and hardly exciting. Yet the subject is anything but just technical, and anything but narrow. Indeed, in these days of still fragile recovery from the financial typhoon that hit East Asia in mid-1997, the subject matter is crucial.

Concerning the *economic context*, the French economist Frederic Bastiat said over a century ago, in his argument against trade protection: "A customs duty is a negative railway." He meant that, by raising the cost of imported goods, tariffs have the exact opposite effect of a new railroad, which lowers transport cost. His story was right, of course, but was not the full story. Economic distance (the difference between the cost at origin and the cost at destination) is a function of *four* elements, not three: insurance, freight, and customs duties, yes, but also the transaction costs generated by cus-

---

* Competent research assistance by Marilyn Pizarro, copy-editing by Mean Asico, and production assistance by Ruby de Vera are gratefully acknowledged. Lorna del Rosario was instrumental in organizing the international seminar on which this volume is based.

1

toms procedures at both ends of the line. Whether embodied in product or packaging modifications, or in time delays, or in "other ways," these transaction costs are real. They are usually accounted for by the exporter and borne by importer and exporter in some proportion to the respective supply and demand elasticities, and entail redistributive effects as well as dead weight economic losses.

In turn, transaction costs themselves comprise costs generated by (i) procedures necessary to protect an identified legitimate public interest (safety, environment, etc.); (ii) customs procedures that are unnecessary or inefficient (or have become so as a result of information technology or other changes); and (iii) bribes or other forms of corruption.

In sum:

The Components of Economic Distance

Economic Distance = Transport + Insurance + Customs
Duties + Transaction Costs

Transaction Costs: = cost of necessary and efficient
customs procedures +
cost of unnecessary or inefficient
customs procedures +
cost of corruption

Accordingly, improvements in customs procedures or removal of unnecessary ones produce at least an unqualified efficiency gain for both the exporter and the importer, *and* an increase in government revenue for the importing country.

Reducing corruption produces an *additional* efficiency and revenue gain and—least measurable but probably most important—a lift in public integrity, which boosts government credibility and produces a positive demonstration effect for other functions of government. As it is unfortunately true that in many countries corruption begins in the customs offices, it is hopefully also true that systemic corruption can be reduced starting from the customs offices themselves.

But procedural improvements and reduced corruption are not independent of each other: on the contrary, common sense and actual experience the world over demonstrate that the single best way to reduce corruption is to streamline the regulations that create opportunities for it.

The simple scheme shown above also brings to light an important consideration. As each of the elements of economic distance is reduced, the others become *relatively* more significant as obstacles to trade. Hence, with the substantial reduction in tariffs over the last two decades, and the further decline in transport and insurance costs, customs procedures have increased in significance. A further boost to international trade can therefore be expected from a major simplification and improvement in customs procedures.

Hence, as summarized below, the simplification and harmonization of customs procedures is directly and closely related to both fiscal policy and governance, as well as to trade expansion.

Simplification and Improvement of Customs Procedures

- Efficiency gain for exporters (profitability of exports increases)
- Efficiency gain for importers (profitability of imports increases)
- Increase in government revenue of importing country
- Fewer opportunities for corruption in customs

Reduction of Corruption in Customs

- Efficiency gain for exporters (increased profitability of exports)
- Efficiency gain for importers (increased profitability of imports)

- Increase in government revenue of importing country
- Improved government integrity and credibility

Overall Impact of Simplification and Improvements in Customs Procedures

- Expanded international trade
- Increased government revenue
- Improved quality of governance

At this point, however, a warning about the nature of institutions and procedural reform is important. Several developing countries have introduced reforms in their customs systems, to the point where the formal system appears robust and coherent in every respect. Yet the efficiency of customs systems remains poor, corruption is endemic, and the quality and timeliness of customs services are no better than they were at the beginning of the "reforms." Why? As illustrated in many of the papers assembled in this book, the answer lies in the nature of institutions.

Colloquially, the term "institution" is used as a synonym for "organization." However, according to the "New Institutional Economics," institutions are best understood as *rules*, and are thus distinct from the organizations that function under them. To use a sports analogy, the sport of tennis is played better or worse depending on the players, but all players must follow the same rules; the "institution" of tennis does not change unless the basic rules are changed (e.g., by removing the net). Customs outcomes are profoundly influenced by customs institutions, i.e., the rules and processes. The problem is that, because institutions comprise both formal and informal rules, many technical "improvements" in the past have failed because they were in conflict with the less visible informal rules and incentives.

Thus, for example, the tendency to underestimate forecasts of customs revenues may stem from concrete incentives to do so rather than from technical weaknesses. Or, in a multi-ethnic country, a performance bonus scheme for customs officials may be perfectly designed on the surface but fail to produce improvements if it is inconsistent with the informal rule that demands that officials use their power to help members of their same ethnic group. Indeed, under these circumstances, the "innovation" may lead to customs officials manipulating customs revenue forecasts and customs rules in the interest of "their" people, and thus to a less efficient system.

The total "stock" of institutions is always larger than is visible on the formal surface, especially in developing countries. This leads to five basic points for customs, among others:

- A design failure that does not take into account key informal rules is likely to lead to a failure of the customs reform itself (to use an analogy, it was the unexposed part of the iceberg that sank the *Titanic*).
- Durable institutional change in general, and in public budgeting in particular, takes a long time to be implemented successfully (a result of what Nobel-prize winner Douglass North called "path dependence").
- One way to improve the *overall* institutional framework is to make the informal rules more visible.
- The media have a key role to play in exploring inefficiencies or malfeasance.
- Customs organizations and new units can be merged, restructured, and recombined, inspection services created, formal penalties increased, and so on—but no change in customs outcomes will result unless the real incentives change as well. Without consequences that are swift, predictable, and uniform (not necessarily heavy), accountability is hollow. And, because most people, including customs officials, are rational, formal improvement in rules and processes without changes in the underlying norms that regulate

behavior will not, of course, change actual behavior. Honest and vigorous new leadership can accomplish a lot in this direction

Finally, there is a general consensus that a country's economic openness to the rest of the world is generally conducive to better economic performance, and that competition can do much for the efficient allocation and use of resources. Simplification of customs procedures is important both for economic openness and for stronger competition.

Concerning *governance*, there is an international consensus, reflected in the ADB Governance Policy of August 1995, that the four key components of governance are accountability, transparency, predictability and participation.

In customs, *accountability* is the capacity to call customs officials to account for their actions. Effective accountability has two components: answerability and consequences. Answerability is the requirement to respond periodically to questions concerning one's official actions. As noted earlier, there is also a need for predictable and meaningful consequences, without which "accountability" is only a time-consuming formality. In addition, both internal (administrative) and external accountability are needed. Particularly with the dramatic improvements in information and communication technology, external accountability through feedback from importers and brokers and the citizenry can now be obtained at low cost by customs officials and is an essential adjunct to improving efficiency and effectiveness of public service delivery. The following papers will pay considerable attention to these new possibilities.

Transparency entails low-cost access to relevant trade and procedural information. This is a must for the public (normally through the filter of capable media). It is essential not only that information be provided, but that it be relevant, understandable, and low-cost. The Internet offers remarkable new possibilities for the low-cost transfer of information.

Predictability results primarily from customs regulations that are clear, known in advance, and uniformly and effectively enforced. Lack of predictability makes it hard for exporters and importers to plan. Predictability of customs decisions is also needed as a signpost on which the private sector can rely to make its own import, marketing, and investment decisions. Most importantly, in order to be predictable, customs regulations must be effectively, fairly, and uniformly applied. Corruption is the most insidious source of unpredictability.

Participation is needed both to obtain reliable information and to serve as a reality check and watchdog for government action. Among other things, participation by external entities is needed as a spur to government operational efficiency, and feedback by users of public services is necessary for monitoring access to and quality of the services. Public/private cooperation is a hallmark of customs improvement and is addressed in several papers in this book.

Part and parcel of the general concern with governance is the new recognition of the costs and inefficiencies of *corruption*. The problem is ancient, and can be found in both the government and the private sector, as recognized in the broad definition of corruption as the "misuse of public or private position for personal gain" adopted in the ADB Anticorruption Policy of July 1998. A balanced approach to combating corruption must therefore address both sides of the equation, and make corruption more difficult and risky for those who would give bribes as well as those who would receive them. The landmark OECD Anti-Bribery Treaty, which was negotiated in December 1997 and came into force February 1999, for the first time makes bribery of a foreign official a crime on a par with bribery of a national official. According to that treaty, if a representative of the exporter bribes a custom official in the importing country, he becomes liable to criminal penalties in *his own country*. Combined with the new consensus on the costs of corruption and convergence of international organization policies, including the ADB and the World Bank, there is now a historic opportunity to reduce corruption radically.

The latest empirical analyses demonstrate that although corruption has complex and varied effects, its negative impact on development is clear.[1] As a result, the environment in which multilateral development banks operate has changed. Pressure for more active measures against bribery and graft is no longer likely to be isolated and sporadic, but has become a systematic feature of the broader debate over good governance and sound development management.

The Bank's anticorruption policy is centered on three objectives:

- supporting competitive markets and efficient, effective, accountable, and transparent public administration, as part of the Bank's broader work on governance;
- supporting promising anticorruption efforts on a case-by-case basis and improving the quality of the Bank's dialogue with its developing member countries (DMCs) on a range of governance issues, including corruption; and
- ensuring that the Bank's projects and staff adhere to the highest ethical standards.

The bulk of the Bank's effort will be directed toward broader measures to improve the quality of governance in the DMCs. This effort will have two components. The first will seek to reduce the scope of direct government intervention in the economy, in the belief that markets should be efficient and competitive, and have as few barriers to entry and exit as possible. This will reduce the opportunity

---

[1] Vito Tanzi, "Governance, Corruption, and Public Finance: An Overview," in *Governance, Corruption, and Public Financial Management*, S. Schiavo-Campo, ed., Asian Development Bank, November 1999, Manila.

for firms or officials to take advantage of artificially restricted markets or suboptimal pricing to demand monopoly rents or bribes.

The second component will focus on supporting improvements in public administration and public-sector management, including customs administration. As mentioned earlier, efforts to simplify customs information systems should improve transparency, accountability, and predictability. Strengthening audit of customs can play the dual role of helping to improve revenue performance while making theft and embezzlement easier to detect. And the streamlining of business processes can improve the efficiency and effectiveness of the public sector while simultaneously reducing opportunities for corruption.

As in the case of poverty, the goal of anticorruption efforts must be defined as *reducing* corruption, not eliminating it (which is impossible) or alleviating it (which is insufficient). However, realistic recognition of the practical difficulties in the struggle against "the cancer of corruption"—as World Bank President James Wolfenson called it in his path-breaking speech at the 1996 Annual meeting of the World Bank and the IMF—must never be allowed to degenerate into shrugging acceptance of this problem. A policy of zero tolerance of corruption is the only defensible and practical policy to minimize actual corruption; tolerance of "minor" thefts has been shown to lead in time to a climate of tolerance of major corruption. This is especially true in customs. (It is crucial, however, to prevent the classic situation where only the "small fish" are caught and penalized).

In closing, simplification of customs procedure is not a narrow technical issue. It represents nothing less than one significant route to improving the quality of governance, which has been shown to be a key factor in efficiency, equity, development, and economic performance. Annexes I and II show a WCO survey of Customs reforms and the UNCTAD trade facilitation recommendations.

The Asia-Europe Meeting (ASEM) was created over three years ago to deal with political, economic, and cultural co-operation issues affecting trade relations between Asia and Europe. Its goal since the start has been to reduce nontariff barriers and enhance trade opportunities between the two regions, complementing the efforts of other international organizations. The first part of the book assembles a comprehensive picture of international efforts at customs simplification by ASEM, APEC and ASEAN, and the World Customs Organization. The second group of papers offers a menu of recent practical initiatives, largely grounded on better public/private cooperation. The last part of the book examines the important case of the airline industry.

Simplification and greater efficiency in customs can also help bring Asia and Europe economically closer together— almost literally so. The stability of the global economic "stool" requires three strong legs: the transpacific leg, the transatlantic leg, and the Asia-Europe leg. The first two legs have been stronger in recent history (although not in earlier historical times). Strengthening the Asia-Europe leg, through trade facilitation that will accompany the simplification of customs procedures on both sides, can play a very important role in attaining sustainable economic growth in Asia and providing a healthy competitive stimulus to Europe.

I: Recent International Initiatives for Customs Simplification

1

Trade Facilitation Efforts of ASEM and Japan

Hiroshi Arichi

The trade facilitation efforts of ASEM and Japan are reflected in the ASEM Trade Facilitation Action Plan (TFAP) and the measures implemented recently by Japan Customs, as described below and summarized in graphic form in annex III.

ASEM Trade Facilitation Action Plan (TFAP)

Background

The Asia-Europe Meeting (ASEM) was launched in Bangkok, Thailand, in March 1996 to address wide-ranging political, economic, and cultural cooperation issues between the two regions.

In view of the importance of trade and investment for sustained economic growth in the ASEM region, the subject has spurred lively discussions from the very beginning. ASEM partners have tackled the matter with a view to reducing nontariff barriers (NTBs) and promoting trade opportunities between the two regions. The intent is to complement, not duplicate, the work being done in bilateral and multilateral forums.

In fact, four months after the inception of ASEM in July 1996, at the first Senior Officials Meeting on Trade and Investment (SOMTI), ASEM members agreed to start developing the TFAP. This was followed by active discussions in various meetings at different levels. A framework for TFAP was approved at the ASEM Economic Ministers Meeting at Makuhari, Japan, in September 1997. In line with this framework, necessary work to specify concrete areas and measures continued. Finally, at the ASEM Summit II in London in April 1998, TFAP was adopted by the ASEM leaders.

The TFAP consists of seven areas: customs procedures; standards, testing, certification, accreditation, and technical regulations; public procurement; quarantine and sanitary and phytosanitary procedures; intellectual property rights; mobility of businesspeople; and other trade activities. The customs procedures area is listed at the top of TFAP.

A question may be raised as to who supervises the TFAP implementation. As a rule, SOMTI, under the ASEM Economic Ministers Meeting, is responsible for supervising TFAP by monitoring progress and ensuring the partners' balanced contribution to this process. SOMTI was requested to submit a report on the progress achieved and additional work required to the Economic Ministers in late 1999 at the Second Economic Ministers Meeting (tentatively set for October 1999 in Berlin, Germany) and before the Third ASEM Summit Meeting in Korea in the year 2000.

To assist SOMTI in these tasks, the TFAP "shepherds" (currently, Korea and the Philippines for the Asian side, and the European Commission and its Presidency [Germany] for the European side) will carry out overall coordination and review. Likewise, to stimulate and coordinate TFAP's implementation, a "facilitator" system was introduced. One partner each from Asia and from Europe was designated for each of the seven TFAP areas. In the case of the customs procedures under TFAP, Japan Customs plays this role for Asia while the European Commission does so for Europe.

Customs areas in TFAP

In response to a call by the ASEM leaders in March 1996, the ASEM Customs Directors-General and Commissioners (DG-C) Meeting was started in June 1996. The objective is to develop closer cooperation among customs authorities in Asia and Europe in customs procedures and the prevention of illegal trafficking of drugs and firearms. The Customs DG-C Meeting has therefore set up two working groups for procedures and enforcement. Although the TFAP process is different from the customs process in that the former is under the ASEM Economic Ministers, the Customs Forum was willing to contribute to the TFAP initiative.

Hence, unlike other TFAP areas, in the case of the customs procedures items in the TFAP the Procedures Working Group coordinates the implementation of the customs areas in the TFAP and reports on its TFAP-related work to SOMTI, as well as to the Customs DG-C Meeting and the ASEM Finance Ministers Meeting.

The main implications of the TFAP are as follows.

1. *Accelerated alignment and harmonization of tariff nomenclature with WCO standards.* This simply means the introduction of the Harmonized System (HS) as the basis for tariff schedules. Nowadays, the HS is widely used and in terms of trade value covers more than 90 percent of international trade. What are the consequences for the private sector? For specific imports, knowing their position in the HS will allow the exact rate of duty in a target market to be determined. HS thus provides transparency and predictability to business and trading circles.

We in customs administrations must admit that there are instances where HS members may classify the same goods in different HS positions. Such cases are settled by the HS committee of the WCO. The WCO has been constantly reviewing and revising the HS to cope with new products appearing in international markets, with changes in trade patterns for internationally traded merchandise, and with requests for subheadings from international organizations. In fact, revisions in the HS for certain headings and subheadings will be finalized within 1999. A similar dialogue would enable ASEM customs to inform the private sector of these changes.

2. *Accelerated implementation of obligations under the WTO Customs Valuation Agreement.* Up to late 1970s, customs valuation was a big headache not only to customs administrations but also to the private sector because of the different sets of customs valuation systems. For instance, it may be easy to say that one has to pay 10 percent or 20 percent as customs duty, but the basis of valuation could differ. Customs value could be based on the CIF (cost, insurance, and freight) principle; on FOB (free on board); on the minimum value set by customs; or on production costs in an importing country.

The Tokyo Round of Multilateral Trade Negotiations worked out the GATT Customs Valuation Code in 1979, which was succeeded in 1995 by the present WTO Customs Valuation Agreement. All developed countries and a number of developing countries now use a uniform basis for assessing the customs value of goods under the "ad valorem" system of rates of duty. The agreement requires WTO members to base customs value on the amount actually paid or payable as normally shown on an invoice.

In this regard, I wish to point out the fact that while most developing countries became members of the WTO in 1995, the WTO Customs Valuation Agreement allows developing member countries a grace period up to five years, until the end of the year 2000, to implement this agreement. In addition, a few ASEM members are now applying for the WTO membership. For these reasons, some Asian members are still in the process of adopting the WTO Customs Valuation Agreement.

What are the benefits of the agreement to the private sector? It simplifies and harmonizes valuation, and gives predictability and transparency to the private sector. The harmonized customs valuation system specified in the agreement uses simplified methods, allowing one to calculate the likely, if not the exact, amount of customs duty.

3. *Efforts to negotiate customs cooperation and mutual administrative assistance agreements between the European Community and the interested ASEM Asian partners.* Customs cooperation and mutual administrative assistance agreements (CMAAs) are directly relevant to customs enforcement rather than to customs procedures and are therefore tackled by another forum, the ASEM Enforcement Working Group.

Consequently, I wish to limit my comments on this. The Enforcement Working Group is actively addressing this important issue. While a CMAA is an agreement between customs authorities, another type of cooperative agreement involves customs administrations and the private sector. In a number of ASEM member countries, a memorandum of understanding (MOU) has been concluded by customs with interested parties in the private sector. Japan Customs has concluded several MOUs with the private sector.

4. *Transparency and predictability.* Transparency can improve through mutual access by ASEM partners to each other's databases (customs duties and nomenclature, tariff quotas, import and export procedures and formalities, rules of origin, customs legislation, etc.). Transparency will also benefit from increased predictability for the business community through the publication and clarification of customs regulations and procedures upon request, taking into account the relevant international customs conventions, such as the Kyoto Convention.

On the issue of mutual access to customs databases, Japan Customs has proposed at the Procedures Working Group to compile a list of such databases to facilitate access not only by ASEM customs authorities but also by the ASEM private sector.

To a greater or lesser extent, ASEM customs administrations have published or are publishing their customs-related laws and regulations and creating a focal point for inquiries. Some members have even started their own customs homepage on the Internet, obviating the need to visit customs offices.

5. *Organization of ASEM seminars for customs and business representatives, in close consultation with the Asia-Europe Business Forum (AEBF).* The seminars would deal with such key issues as risk analysis, EDI, paperless systems, and faster customs handling. This initiative was first put forward by Japan at the First Procedures Working Group meeting in March 1997. With the cooperation of ADB and the Philippine Customs Authority, the first such seminar took place in February 1999 at the ADB Headquarters in Manila. The seminar provided an opportunity to discuss where ASEM customs authorities are headed and what the private sector would like them to consider in respect of trade facilitation. Seminar participants from the private sector and customs gained much information and a deeper understanding of the customs agenda for the future. We should seek ways to follow through these activities by focusing more on specific areas.

6. *Promotion of standardized and simplified documentation taking international standards and the ongoing discussions in various international forums into account.* This is, in fact, both a new and an old issue. We have made an effort in various international forums to standardize customs documents. Although it would be ideal to have a standard import declaration form, for example, we also have to be realistic in addressing this issue. As you can imagine, each customs agency is tasked with a different set of responsibilities and competence such that the entry items in a declaration can differ from one customs agency to another. Thus, standardizing the import declaration form is not easy.

As a pragmatic approach and while allowing some flexibility to customs administrations, customs forums such as the WCO and the G7 Customs Experts Group have been taking steps to promote standardized and simplified documentation in the context of revisions in the Kyoto Convention and the establishment of a data set for customs clearance.

7. *Where appropriate, the exploration of possible common positions for ASEM partners in WTO and WCO.* This particular item is on the agenda of the Third Procedures Working Group meeting, and I do not wish to preempt the discussion. However, I can say at this point that it would be beneficial for us to at least exchange views on negotiating customs issues to build a consensus in the WTO and the WCO, taking into account different national interests in ASEM customs administrations.

8. *Technical assistance and training programs related to simplified customs procedures.* Such programs will contribute to ASEM expertise and experience and to the achievement of the deliverables discussed above. But there are several bottlenecks. For example, within ASEM, we have no established funds available for customs areas. We, the developed ASEM customs members, have sufficient expertise and experience to assist developing members. However, we have limited financial resources for technical assistance. Under these circumstances, I suggest that we could look into the possibility of providing assistance upon request by ASEM customs administrations as part of existing technical assistance and training projects and programs. Another possibility would be for the ASEM private sector to jointly sponsor an activity of your priority customs area or areas.

Let me next take this opportunity to briefly touch on the trade facilitation efforts of my administration in Japan.

Japan's Trade Facilitation Initiatives

Survey on the time required for the release of goods

Customs has two contradictory missions: enforcement and trade facilitation. One of our important tasks at the central administration level is to achieve a right balance between these two, bearing in mind the need and requests from the public and private sectors. This is not an easy task.

With regard to trade facilitation, which is the main theme of this seminar, Japan Customs in 1991 started a survey on the time required for the release of goods. This survey was made right after the trade talks between Japan and the United States, to arrive at an objective measure of progress toward trade facilitation. So far, we have had five surveys, the last one in 1998.

This survey focuses on the average time from the arrival of cargo to its release. After each survey, we hold a hearing at which various import-related associations and companies are encouraged to present ideas and comments on the causes of the delay. Actions have been taken to reduce the impediments disclosed by the survey and the hearing.

As a result, we have substantially reduced the time required for the release of goods. The first survey in 1991 revealed that the average time required for the release of cargoes was 2.3 hours for air cargoes and 26.1 hours for sea cargoes. In the 1988 survey, the time had been dramatically reduced to 0.7 hours for air cargoes (a reduction of 70 percent) and to 5.6 hours for sea cargoes (a reduction of 79 percent).

Most of the reduction in the time required for the release of air cargoes took place between 1996 and 1998, when the time dropped by 60 percent, from 1.8 hours to 0.7 hours. This significant reduction, according to our analysis, was mainly due to a special customs procedure for immediate release upon arrival and computer networking with quarantine offices and other agencies.

In the case of sea cargoes, the time required for their release also shortened significantly, by 45 percent, from 10.2 hours in 1996 to 5.6 hours in 1998. The main reasons for the reduction were wider use of a pre-arrival examination system and the introduction of computer networking with other agencies as well as a computerized customs clearance system for air cargoes called Air NACCS (Nippon Automated Cargo Clearance System).

*Other recent initiatives of Japan Customs to simplify and
harmonize customs procedures*

Japan Customs has been implementing other initiatives
to further reduce the time for customs clearance for trade
facilitation. For instance, we have expanded the coverage of
NACCS, which is now used not only in major ports and airports but also in a number of small-and-medium size ports
and airports. In 1998, it was used to process more than 90
percent of total import declarations.

As I have mentioned, the necessary formalities at a port
involve not only customs but also other agencies and ministries. Having electronically interfaced authorities certainly
reduces the time required. NACCS is now interfaced with
other online systems that deal with other import requirements such as quarantines and food sanitation administered
by other ministers. This interface has helped speed up trade
procedures.

As for imported cargoes processed through Air-NACCS,
a "special customs procedure for immediate release on arrival"
has been introduced and has facilitated customs clearance.
In the case of export declarations, we have introduced a simplified documentation system for clearance whereby invoices
or airway bills are accepted as substitutes for export declaration.

Furthermore, to maximize the use of information technology, Japan Customs has opened a homepage, both in Japanese and in English, to spread customs-related information.
Advance classification ruling through the Internet has also
just begun.

Future initiatives

Finally, I would like to mention a couple of measures
that Japan Customs plans to take to further reduce the time
required for customs clearance.

The current Sea-NACCS will be upgraded within 1999,
not to curtail the necessary clearance but to speed up the

release of goods by doing away with unnecessary stages in the process. An amendment to the NACCS law is now being discussed in the Diet. We also plan to expand the interface network to process requirements under the Foreign Exchange and Foreign Trade Control Law. Once these plans are realized, Japan Customs will be able to process the whole range of import/export procedures, from the arrival of vessels to the release of import cargoes, and from the arrival of export cargoes at customs bonded areas to the departure of the carrying vessels.

2

The World Customs Organization and Trade Facilitation

Rob van Kuik

The Convention establishing the Customs Cooperation Council was signed in Brussels in 1950. Since 1994, the organization has been known as the World Customs Organization (WCO). The change in name reflects the fact that the organization is no longer an inner circle of customs administrations working together among themselves but one that is more open to implementing WTO trade policy and interacting with clients/partners in the business community. In short, the change in name symbolizes a clear shift in the mentality of customs.

The WCO and many national customs administrations are trying their best to promote and not to hinder international trade. Their efforts are, however, mostly limited to their direct area of competence, in particular customs procedures and the related control methods. Where national customs administrations act on behalf of other ministries (other than the ministry of finance or trade to which they are normally connected), more effort will be needed to attain further simplification and global harmonization. It would be helpful if the customs agency were to be increasingly recognized as the sole government agency that deals with international goods traffic.

To give a global perspective to WCO efforts to further facilitate international trade, the following discussion is centered on these topics: technical work, enforcement, customs reform and modernization, customs integrity, use of information technology, and revision of the Kyoto Convention.

Technical Work

The WCO is a technical, broadly nonpolitical organization that has achieved great success in its simplification and harmonization efforts through effective technical work for trade facilitation. Examples of its valuable technical work are:

- The United Nations, through its facilitation committee CEFACT, is drafting a recommendation to promote the use of the Harmonized System (HS), a logical classification system for the description and coding of goods, in all phases of international trade and transportation. The HS is constantly being updated. The latest update was approved in June 1999 for implementation by the almost 100 contracting parties (CPs) by January 1, 2002.
- The GATT Valuation Code has replaced earlier principles of customs valuation. The customs value is no longer attached to the "normal price" concept. Instead, the transaction value (invoice price) is now used unless there are serious reasons against it. Forty-nine CPs have adopted this new mode of valuation, with fifty-six more to follow, based on their WTO commitments.
- Potentially a third success is the harmonization of rules for nonpreferential origin, which has been entrusted by the WTO to the WCO. This work has not kept to the original time schedule probably because it is more political rather than technical in nature. Still, it is hoped that WCO will be able to finish the work by the end of 1999.

Enforcement

Customs has the dual task of:

- ensuring the correct calculation and payment of customs duties and taxes on imports and exports; and
- enforcing prohibitions, restrictions, and control measures on specific goods.

Enforcement is often regarded as an internal customs activity. The Netherlands, however, has always stressed that enforcement and simplification of customs procedures are very closely related. Procedures can be simplified only if effective customs enforcement capabilities are in place. On the other hand, enforcement, which protects bona fide companies from unfair competition, is also easier if procedures are simpler.

In today's global marketplace, customs administrations need to cooperate more closely with one another to carry out their tasks in an efficient and effective manner. WCO plays an important role in this respect as in the following four examples:

- Regional Intelligence Liaison Offices, a global customs network;
- WCO databases;
- bilateral agreements; and
- multilateral agreements (Nairobi Convention).

Memorandums of Understanding have also been drawn up between the WCO and international business associations, national customs administrations and their associations, and individual companies to strengthen cooperation, improve customs enforcement, and facilitate international trade. Business circles supply pre-arrival information on goods to customs for better-targeted control on the basis of risk analysis.

Business thus benefits from minimized customs intervention in the flow of goods. The WCO's ACTION/DEFIS program promotes this concept of cooperation.

Customs Reform and Modernization

Efficient and effective customs administration is another important prerequisite for the smooth flow of goods. Even the most advanced procedure can be frustrated by inefficient application and control. The goal is to make customs administrations more self-reliant in:

- constantly adapting to changes in the environment;
- making better use of resources;
- strengthening their management and human resource capabilities; and
- delivering effective and efficient service.

Customs Integrity

The fact that the integrity problem in customs is now openly discussed shows how much customs has opened up to the outside world. In the 1993 Arusha Declaration, Directors-General and Commissioners of Customs underscored the importance of the issue. Business circles quite rightly expect a high level of integrity from customs just as they do from police or judicial authorities. But this problem will remain intractable as long as working conditions in the country (including salaries and career prospects) remain poor and corruption is commonplace.

Like inefficiency, corruption can effectively hinder trade because it renders clearance times and costs uncertain for business. Following a symposium last year where the importance of the issue was emphasized, the WCO is considering drafting an Integrity Action Plan.

Use of Information Technology (IT)

The use of information technology facilitates customs clearance. However, to simplify the underlying procedures true facilitation is needed. Some examples of the WCO's work in this field are:

- seamless data flow—one-time lodging of data, as in the US/UK prototyping;
- efforts to develop a methodology for unique consignment codes;
- WCO common customs data model (based on the G7 initiative to reduce customs data requirements); and
- WCO Data Mapping Guide to ensure consistency in the use of UN/EDIFACT in customs messages.

Revision of the Kyoto Convention

The original (1973) Kyoto Convention was aimed to bring about a global simplification and harmonization of customs procedures but had a number of inherent weaknesses. It was constituted of a "body" describing e.g. the formalities on how to become contracting party and of 31 Annexes on specific customs procedures, each one consisting of standards and recommended practices. Under the Convention it was possible to become a contracting party (CP) to the Kyoto Convention by accepting the body and only one of the Annexes. Furthermore CP's could enter reservations in respect of any provision that they did not want to accept. This procedure made it possible to become a CP as a political gesture but without changing anything in the country's customs legislation or practice.

By contrast, the revised Kyoto Convention comprises next to the body of the Convention, a horizontal Annex and 10 specific Annexes. In order to become a CP the horizontal Annex and one specific Annex have to be accepted. No reservations are allowed any more to standards although there are some transitional standards (which may be implemented over a period after acceptance). Furthermore, the revised Convention contains more detail in the annexes as well as guidelines for implementation to avoid misunderstandings about their exact meaning. Now that the revision is agreed, there is a need for all present CPs to accept and implement the provisions of the revised Convention. Secondly, a much broader acceptance is needed than the present range of contracting parties.

Only global and uniform application of the simplified customs procedures will really help the private sector to reduce costs and will foster world trade. Outside support to stimulate acceptance by countries will be very welcome. For instance WTO could provide such support.

Conclusion

This paper has been limited to a discussion of highlights of the WCO work program, which has a much wider scope. Nonetheless, it can be gleaned from the points brought out here that WCO and customs administrations in general are opening up to the outside world. They have come to realize that they have direct influence only on customs procedures, and that they must therefore strengthen their ties with international business and international organizations to achieve the overall goal of trade facilitation.

3

Activities of the Asia-Pacific Economic Cooperation Forum

Ibrahim bin Md. Isa

This paper relates efforts of the Asia-Pacific Economic Cooperation-Subcommittee on Customs Procedures (APEC-SCCP) forum to simplify and harmonize customs procedures particularly during the years 1997 and 1998.

The SCCP was established in 1994 to carry out the decisions of APEC leaders and ministers in customs matters. In particular, it pursues efforts to simplify and harmonize customs procedures and ultimately to facilitate trade between APEC countries, as outlined in the trade and investment framework.

Efforts of the SCCP

The SCCP first identified potential action plans and then decided on 12 collective action plans (CAPs) with agreed target dates. These CAPs are as follows:

- Harmonization of the Tariff Structure with the Harmonized System (HS) Convention;
- Public Availability of Information on Customs Laws, Regulations, Administrative Guidelines, and Rulings;
- Simplification and Harmonization on the Basis of the Kyoto Convention;
- Adoption and Support of the UN/EDIFACT;
- Adoption of the Principles of the WTO Valuation Agreement;

- Adoption of the Principles of the WTO Intellectual Property Rights Agreement;
- Introduction of a Clear Appeal Provision;
- Introduction of an Advance Classification Ruling System;
- Provisions for Temporary Importation;
- Harmonized APEC Data Elements;
- Risk Management Techniques; and
- Guidelines on Express Consignments Clearance.

The SCCP is also working on other initiatives (strategic business partnership, E-commerce, advance passenger clearance, APEC business card for business and traveler mobility, tariff database, etc.) with the same objective of simplifying and harmonizing customs procedures.

Coordinators have been assigned to monitor and report on the progress of implementation of the CAPs and to evaluate the results. Among their other duties, they submit funding proposals to the APEC Budget and Management Committee for technical assistance for the CAPs. The coordinators will also work with volunteer economists in preparing training modules and organizing field trips for assessment, advisory, training, and other purposes.

Furthermore, in an extension of the implementation of CAPs at the national level each country will plan its own course of action and implement each CAP item accordingly, to achieve the intended results by the target dates. For best results, technical assistance in the implementation of these individual action plans (IAPs) must be delivered efficiently and effectively. It is thus essential that both the recipient and the donor economies cooperate closely and be totally committed.

Implementation of CAPs

A discussion of the implementation of some of the CAPs will show what the SCCP is doing to simplify and harmonize customs procedures. Starting with five CAPs items in

1997, the SCCP implemented three more CAPs in 1998. Most of these are being implemented in stages, and require sustained efforts. Obviously, this means that cost and time are important considerations.

The CAP for the Adoption of the Principles of the WTO Valuation Agreement is one such multiphased program. Technical assistance is being provided in stages, and covers a wide range of issues and activities. Among these is the legislative framework creating the organization, setting up clearance and verification procedures, and providing for the valuation and training needs.

Phase 1 involved information gathering and confirmation of the needs of the recipient economies. In phase 2, experts from member countries such as Australia, Canada, New Zealand, and the US conducted training workshops in nine member countries from October to December 1997. Workshops for training needs analysis were also completed at about the same time, under phase 3. Also in 1997, training courses in basic WCO customs valuation were held in two countries under phase 4 of the program. The total budget approved by the APEC Trade and Investment Liberalization and Facilitation (TILF) Fund for this project in 1997 was US$468,380.

A three-module advanced training program was developed in 1998. Delivery of the first module, which focused on the valuation task forces in the implementing member countries, began in 1998 and is continuing in 1999.

Another CAP that was first implemented in 1997 and is continuing in 1999 is the Introduction of an Advance Classification Ruling System. As in the other CAP, the specific needs of the recipient countries were initially assessed through missions and questionnaires. Training formats or guidelines were prepared on the basis of the needs analysis.

Two experts each from the US and Malaysia delivered the technical assistance training program to the recipient countries in Manila in October–November 1997. The technical assistance for Taipei, China was to have been delivered in 1998 but was postponed to March 1999. Possibly, Papua New Guinea will also receive technical assistance this year.

The Guidelines for Express Consignments Clearance were the subject of one of the three new items that were added to the list of CAPs in 1997. The coordinators for this project worked closely with the International Express Carriers Conference (IECC) and the Conference of Asia-Pacific Express Carriers (CAPEC). Specific principles that have been identified so far by member countries include the establishment of minimum facilitative clearance procedures for low-value shipments, risk assessment, and hours of operations suited to business needs.

The implementation of one CAP—Public Availability of Information on Customs Laws, Regulations, Administrative Guidelines, and Rulings—is deemed complete. The coordinators have compiled a handbook of best practices in SCCP member countries in disseminating customs information to the public. This publication is also available on the SCCP Web site at www.sccp.org/frames-library.htm. Nevertheless, efforts to enhance and improve information dissemination will continue.

At the micro level, among the IAPs that are being implemented by individual countries is the Malaysian program involving electronic data interchange in the import and export process. In fact, Malaysia preempted the SCCP decision on the UN/EDIFACT CAPs item when it became the first to introduce a proprietary system known as *sistem maklumat kastam-dagang net* (SMK* Dagangnet) in 1995. This system enables the customs administration to process import and export transactions electronically, from the submission of import/export documents to the final release from customs, and including the payment of duties, fees, and other related charges through electronic funds transfer. What needs to be done next is probably to realign the proprietary system with the UN electronic messaging format for automated systems.

Strategic Partnership Between Customs and Industry

To further enhance the implementation of CAPs, the SCCP is cooperating with business to develop a modern customs framework which fits the needs of business. To this end, the SCCP has developed the Guidelines for SCCP and Business Strategic Partnerships, which govern the involvement of business in the SCCP CAP and other initiatives.

To date, several successful partnerships with business have been formed. Industry has provided the SCCP with valuable technical expertise and financial assistance on some CAP projects, as well as offers of assistance in the form of computers and other goods.

In the matter of business funding of SCCP activities, the SCCP has gone one step further and developed a simple mechanism for administering funding offers from business. Members feel the funds received should be managed by an independent body to avoid conflict of interest. As such, they agreed to set up a trust fund to be managed by the APEC Secretariat. Contributors would deposit their funds with the Secretariat which would then make disbursements in accordance with the SCCP requirements.

Finally, to strengthen communication with industry, the SCCP has developed the SCCP Web site and organized the so-called APEC Customs-Industry Dialogue which is held annually in conjunction with the SCCP meetings.

II: Improving Service and Efficiency in Customs

4

The Role of the World Trade Organization

Hans Van Bodegraven

The International Context

Over the last 50 years, we have witnessed a tremendous increase in international trade. Today we live in a global marketplace where optimal allocation of resources is a key activity. Unprecedented developments in transport, such as containerization, computerization, speed, and just-in-time delivery and other new logistic concepts have enabled companies to cope with this global marketplace.

Another important contribution to the enormous growth in international trade is the globalization of production and the steady rise in the international movements of goods and services within multinational companies; one-third of movements of international goods are intracompany transactions.

Present global trade patterns show that the business community, by engaging in international trade, is very aware of its possibilities. However, notwithstanding its enormous growth, international trade is far from being unhampered. Providing the data necessary for the movement of goods across borders, such as all kinds of certificates and documents, proofs of origin, and invoices, accounts for an estimated 2–10 percent of the final market price of the goods concerned in the country of destination.

It is the consumers who finally pick up the bill for these costs. Not only will they have to pay the extra costs, they also cannot profit from the full benefits which an open market can give them. According to some estimates, reducing or eliminating these costs could mean a cost saving of up to US$75 billion worldwide and could give an important boost to the world economy, particularly welcome in these times of economic crisis in Asia, Russia, and Latin America.

Relationship Between Trade Facilitation and Customs Procedures

Customs procedures, in spite of the great efforts to simplify and harmonize them, are still the most visible barriers to international trade. At the same time, these procedures remain very important in the context of revenue collection and the protection of society.

Trade facilitation in general can be defined in many ways. According to one definition, which is incorporated in the mission statement of the United Nations–Centre for the Facilitation of Procedures and Practices for Administration, Commerce and Transport (UN CEFACT), trade facilitation consists of:

> activities dedicated to improving the ability of business, trade and administrative organizations, from developed, developing and transitional economies to exchange products and relevant services effectively.

It is clear from this definition that (as also explained in the Introduction) the simplification and harmonization of customs procedures is an important part of this much broader aim. Since duties and tariffs have been reduced, customs procedures and practices as such are mentioned increasingly as the main remaining barriers to world trade. The initiatives taken by the customs community itself, especially revising the WCO Kyoto Convention, the main international instrument dealing with customs procedures, will only partly solve the problem. The customs community cannot take away the underlying political and legal differences between states in the fields of trade, agriculture, safety, public order, etc. There we enter the much wider world of international trade policy.

I will therefore focus my presentation on the links between trade policy in general and simplification and harmonization of customs procedures. I will then turn to the question of which international organization the Netherlands considers to be best equipped to deal with these politically sensitive issues. This question is very topical because of the present discussions on the scope of the Millennium Round negotiations in the World Trade Organization.

I will first give you a brief overview of the existing barriers to international trade and the role of customs in trade facilitation and then turn to the WTO.

Barriers to International Trade

After the substantive tariff reductions in earlier rounds of GATT negotiation, further reductions may be expected during the forthcoming Millennium Round. The more tariffs are reduced, the more attention will focus on remaining barriers to international trade. Whether clearly visible or hidden, these barriers still cover a very wide range.

Not all of them can, by the way, be linked to government regulations. For instance, some of the banking requirements, such as some forms of documentary credits dependent on original paper documents and insurance of international transport, can effectively discourage small- and medium-sized companies in particular from exploring foreign markets.

International business has over the years learned to cope with the remaining barriers. At the same time, we should realize that most of the small- and medium-sized companies do not have the resources needed to overcome these barriers. They are therefore forced to compete in foreign markets at substantially higher cost than local competitors and will very often simply refrain from going beyond their local market. To put it in simple terms: international trade is at present so much more complicated than national trade that many companies simply do not bother to look beyond national borders. This is particularly true for companies from least developed and developing countries and for small- and medium-sized companies.

Possible Role of Customs

The role of customs is important, but limited by its nature. Customs does not make policies, but enforces laws regarding the cross-border flow of goods. By the nature of this task, customs is often blamed for the delays caused by government regulations. To make things more complicated, in practice import/export legislation is often enforced by a range of specialized control agencies which require completely different data sets, procedures, and practices. This uncoordinated government intervention sometimes leads to extreme holding times at the border crossing points.

Within its limits in the recent past, customs has contributed a lot to reducing the barriers. As examples of measures that have facilitated international trade considerably I would just like to mention the harmonized system for the description and coding of goods and the Kyoto Convention on the simplification and harmonization of customs procedures. The use of electronic data processing techniques has also helped traders to deal with customs procedures.

In the future, customs can play a role in lowering the barriers, first by introducing the new Kyoto Convention as soon as possible and by starting new initiatives in the field of international cooperation. But customs might, for instance, also get the primary responsibility for dealing with cross-border traffic of goods (front-line agency). Customs should therefore be consulted whenever new legislative measures in respect of cross-border traffic are being considered.

Customs might also be given the role of coordinating the activities of other control agencies involved in order to avoid accumulating handling delays for a single consignment (single-window/one-stop clearance). This presupposes that customs also has to be the central agency to receive the data concerning this international traffic of goods prior to the arrival of the goods for risk assessment. This would enable customs to clear goods before their arrival in the customs territory. Benefits may also be derived from prototype projects wherein export data may serve as import data in the country of destination.

The efforts of customs in trade facilitation will, however, always be limited to issues in their area of competence. Many of the barriers to international trade are controlled or enforced by customs, but not decided upon by customs. As a first step toward removing these barriers, the whole range of obstacles should be reviewed from a political standpoint. Therefore, an international political framework is urgently needed.

The Forum Best Equipped to Deal with Trade Facilitation

Discussions on aspects of trade facilitation take place in many specialized or regional forums, such as G7, APEC, ASEM, ASEAN, NAFTA, and the possible future FTAA. Other international organizations like WCO, IMO, ICAO, ICS, IATA, ICC also deal with aspects of trade facilitation. Without a detailed analysis of the work programs of all of these organizations, I think it is true to say that their efforts result in many positive initiatives, but the overall effect is limited because the results are not coordinated and not universally adaptable or enforceable.

European experience in the past two decades shows that to eliminate international trade barriers effectively, a firm political decision has to be taken. One should recall that in

1986, in the so-called white paper on the completion of the internal market, an inventory among EU member states showed an impressive list of over 400 legislative or regulatory differences between EU member states requiring as many customs controls at their internal frontiers. These differences made it impossible to create a real internal market.

A firm decision was therefore taken by the European Council to harmonize the legislative measures concerned. By 1993, these differences had disappeared. Consequently, all customs controls at the internal frontiers could be abolished and the internal market, although not quite achieved yet, could at least function without physical controls on goods at the borders.

The lesson to draw from this is that genuine political commitment around the world is needed for the effective reduction of barriers to international trade. The present discussions, for example in the G7, on the reduction of data requirements in cross-border traffic of goods at best serve as a technical input in discussions at the global level. Trade facilitation is not a matter for just an élite group of seven economic superpowers; it can and will be achieved only when all states, including the least developed countries, see the benefits of further facilitation and agree to eliminate barriers.

The most likely forum for obtaining the necessary global consensus is, in my opinion, the World Trade Organization.

WTO Involvement in Trade Facilitation

The Uruguay Round has brought about a fundamental change in international trade policy. After the earlier multilateral trade negotiations had only imposed rather limited commitments and had not engaged many developing countries, the Marrakesh agreements have strengthened the international economic institutional framework considerably.

In particular, the fact that the World Trade Organization has been given wide-ranging supervisory powers, an effective procedure for dispute settlement, and the power to lay down binding rules, has changed the international environment considerably.

The WTO does have some experience in the field of customs. As an example, I would like to mention the GATT Valuation Code which was an important step forward compared with the classical method of calculating the customs value of goods. The code is being introduced by many countries and constitutes an important step forward in worldwide standard customs procedures. In 95–99 percent of cases (or even more), the invoice value will be used. Only in case of well-founded doubt can the invoice price be challenged. This means that the importers concerned can predict much more the amount of duties payable and that there will be less reason for disputes and resulting delays.

Secondly, carrying out the GATT-Uruguay agreement in this area, the WTO launched a process to harmonize the rules for determination of the nonpreferential origin which are used in the application of various trade-policy instruments. In view of the available expertise there, the technical discussion of this matter has been assigned to the World Customs Organization (WCO), in particular the Technical Committee on Rules of Origin (TCRO). Results reached by the TCRO (Brussels) are submitted to the Committee on Rules of Origin (CRO) in Geneva for political endorsement. The process is to be finalized before the Ministerial Conference which is planned for the end of 1999.

In sharp contrast to the deliberately low political profile of the WCO, the WTO is a highly political organization. It is now recognized as *the* international authority to discuss matters of international trade policy and has shown great influence in recent years.

Since the WTO is the only global organization dealing with trade policy matters in a broad sense and has a high political profile, it is in principle very well suited to dealing with trade facilitation issues. Of course, the organization does not have the technical expertise to deal with the very wide variety of trade barriers under discussion. It should certainly be backed up with the technical expertise of other organizations such as the WCO for customs-related items.

Another organization that could, in my view, play an important supporting role is UN/CEFACT. This UN body deals in particular with the facilitation of procedures and practices in administration, commerce, and transport. There is an impressive list of UN recommendations that could play a role in the present efforts.

In a first informal symposium held in March 1998, a great number of topics in the field of trade facilitation were mentioned that could be tackled in the Millennium Round. I would like to highlight a couple of points most relevant to customs:

- reducing and simplifying documentation and data for export and import purposes;
- harmonizing documents and data requirements with internationally agreed standards such as those of the United Nations;
- allowing the electronic generation and submission of reduced and internationally harmonized trade documentation; and
- introducing modern customs procedures, including risk assessment, pre-arrival processing, audit-based controls, fast-track clearance for authorized traders, acceptance of export data at import, concentration of all official controls in the hands of customs (one-stop clearance), and customs integrity.

I would like to stress in this context that the present revision of the Kyoto Convention will be an extremely important step in the right direction as far as customs procedures in the strict sense are concerned. I should add, however, that the Kyoto Convention is not the panacea for all problems related to customs that some people believe it to be. For example, the Kyoto Convention will not solve existing ineffi- ciencies in the organization of customs administrations, ri- valry between official control agencies, or problems of integrity. Only a well-balanced reform and modernization program, together with the necessary funds to implement the recom- mendations, will solve these more fundamental problems.

Upcoming WTO Ministerial Conference

The Ministerial Conference of the WTO to be held at the end of 1999 will decide on the exact scope of the Millennium negotiations. Trade facilitation must be one of the topics for the negotiations. Given the close relationship between trade facilitation and customs-related topics, facilitation of customs procedures should be high on the priority list.

General support from the WTO for the worldwide accept- ance and implementation of the revised Kyoto Convention would be most welcome. I can also see benefit in WTO support for broad initiatives in the field of reform and modernization of customs administrations and for the systematic examina- tion of the range of barriers to trade, with the assistance of specialized agencies such as UN/CEFACT and WCO.

WTO State of Affairs with Regard to Trade Facilitation

Four informal meetings and the symposium mentioned earlier have been held so far, resulting in recommendations from the Council of Trade in Goods to the ministerial con- ference to be held at the end of the year.

The positions in Geneva are not completely clear. It looks like all developed countries are now convinced of the need to tackle trade facilitation in the Millennium negotiations and at least to lay down some guiding principles for trade facili- tation and to create a framework in which trade facilitation can be dealt with in a consistent and coherent way.

It is remarkable that some of the less developed countries seem a little hesitant to recognize that trade facilitation could be beneficial to all countries. It is generally accepted that the creation of an open-market economy allowing optimal allocation of resources is one of the best ways to contribute to and to profit from economic development.

Open markets can, however, function properly only if procedures designed to facilitate the flow of goods are put in place and the regulatory capacity of the country concerned is made effective. In particular, lowering the present threshold for engaging in international trade, caused by unclear procedures among other things, would likely benefit companies from developing countries in particular, and could lead to substantial growth in their exports. Similarly, lowering barriers to imports will inevitably lead to more competition and better allocation of resources on the local markets in developing countries.

Of course, any new WTO activities in the field of trade facilitation must also have an impact on existing agreements such as the agreements on import licensing procedures, on preshipment inspections, on technical barriers to trade, and on sanitary and phytosanitary measures. A critical examination of all these existing instruments should be part of the WTO activities in the field of trade facilitation.

The EU and Dutch Positions

An important input so far in the inventory of possible trade facilitation issues for the Millennium Round negotiations has come from the European Union. The overriding message in the European contributions is that trade facilitation in the end benefits all states around the world and suits both international business circles and governments. It will open markets that are now in fact effectively closed, in particular for small- and medium-sized companies.

At the same time, reducing barriers will open up markets for business from developing countries because of substantially less investment needed to cope with procedures elsewhere. To quote the Ministerial Declaration on Trade efficiency of October 1994:

> Greater participation in international trade is a prerequisite for development. Dynamic and healthy international trade is a major instrument for the economic growth and sustainable development of countries. It also contributes to the goals of poverty alleviation and employment creation on a worldwide basis.

In its latest contribution to the WTO debate, the European Union has stressed the need to include concrete commitments for capacity building in developing countries. In February 1999 there was a broad consultation of Dutch international business circles about their expectations and wishes in respect of the WTO activities in the field of trade facilitation. The meeting showed clear support for the view adopted by the European Union that, based on present status and past experience, the WTO is the best political forum to reach progress on a future strategy for trade facilitation.

Conclusions

The key conclusions are as follows:

- Trade facilitation is an extremely important instrument for the further growth of the world economy, and presents a win-win situation for developed countries, developing countries, and countries in transition.
- The WTO is the international organization best suited to achieve real progress in the field of trade facilitation. Restricted, regional, or specific organizations can only play a supportive role.

- The Millennium Round should cover the broadest possible range of topics.
- The WTO should be assisted in this challenging task by the WCO and UN CEFACT.
- The specific customs administrative input in the discussion on trade facilitation should focus on:
  - acceptance of the revised Kyoto Convention;
  - initiatives beyond the provisions of the Kyoto Convention (single-window/one-stop, prototyping, etc.);
  - the reform and modernization program; and
  - the principles of the Arusha Declaration.

5

A Customs System for Improved Service and Efficiency

Patrick Heinesson

Swedish Customs

G reat changes have come over Swedish Customs in re cent years.[1] New rules have been introduced in conjunction with Sweden's accession to the European Union (EU). To meet EU requirements, Swedish Customs has changed its work methods, chiefly through increasingly integrated IT operations. The goal is to be regarded as the most efficient in Europe, in both service and information to industry and in the fight against illegal imports of narcotics, alcohol, and cigarettes.

The business concept it has adopted calls for Swedish Customs to offer the following:

- flexible customs routines within the framework of foreign trade regulations;
- simple border passage for travelers and efficient border protection;
- constant improvement of customs routines to benefit the public to the greatest possible extent and to strengthen Swedish competitiveness; and
- cooperation with industry and other authorities.

---

[1] From Kjell Jansson, Director-General for Customs, "New Swedish Customs," a report, January 1999.

Swedish Customs seeks to play a major role in border protection and to reduce by 25 percent the social costs of illegal imports of narcotics, alcohol, and tobacco. It also looks forward to collaborating with industry and to receiving high-quality declarations, 90 percent of which will not require manual handling. In the field of national and international cooperation, Swedish Customs wants to be known for progressive thinking, work simplification, and development of work methods.

The ten-point change program of Swedish Customs is summarized below:

- *Comprehensive view.* Swedish Customs must be organized and its work methods formulated to create a common approach that is conducive to public benefit, efficiency, and customer orientation.
- *Readiness for change.* Through systematic change, the organization and the work methods will be formulated and adapted to suit new global requirements and the demands of efficient operations.
- *Strategic work.* Organizational strategies and vision will be given high priority.
- *Development.* Development of work methods and IT- and technology-based procedures, as well as training, will be a main strategic task and an integral part of operations.
- *Cooperation and collaboration.* Central and regional units will cooperate within and among themselves, and will work in such a way as to facilitate and encourage collaboration with other nationally and international authorities.
- *Uniformity.* Regulations and work routines will be uniformly applied throughout the organization and operations of Swedish Customs.
- *Structure.* The organization will adopt a geographic and reporting structure that accords with the nature of its

business and the efficient distribution of its resources.

- *Management and control.* Strategic management and control of operations will be clear and coherent.
- *Work methods and work forms.* Swedish Customs will organize itself for its ongoing projects and devise new work forms to be able to use its resources efficiently, achieve flexibility and mobility, and muster strength.
- *Process orientation.* Swedish Customs will have a process-oriented organization and will operate in accordance with its two main processes, Managing the Trade and Border Protection.

Processes of Swedish Customs

A process orientation is needed to reflect the importance of each part of the operation to the vision and the overall goals of the organization. The two main operational processes of Swedish Customs are Managing the Trade and Border Protection. There are two supporting processes: Analysis and Crime Investigation.

Managing the Trade is the handling of commercial goods traffic. It applies quality assurance in order to develop and sustain Swedish Customs as an efficient link in the foreign-trade chain and to promote revenue collection and foreign trade documentation within the framework of given restrictions. The process starts outside Swedish Customs when a company expresses interest in importing, exporting, or transiting a commodity and is completed when the correct revenue has been handed over to the government.

Border Protection is concerned with the handling of illegal traffic. Its purpose is to prevent unwanted goods from crossing the border. The process starts with the prevention of smuggling and ends when control and evaluation are completed and possibly a crime has been reported.

The National Risk Analysis Program

For the past few years, the Swedish Customs has been developing a range of work methods to facilitate foreign trade and to rationalize its own procedures. Applying risk analysis to customs procedures, for instance, has proved useful in determining the facilities that may be granted to individual economic operators.

Thanks to the computerized Customs Information System (TDS), which has been adopted nationwide, over 70 percent of customs declarations are now submitted to Customs in paperless form (EDI). A computerized risk analysis system is also being developed to help identify, manage, and control high-risk areas, while allowing automatic customs clearance to low-risk entries.

In October 1996, the Swedish Board of Customs started a project named RISK to study and implement new working methods. The project was carried out in three stages: study (October 1996 to May 1997), design (April to December 1997), and implementation (January to December 1998). In May 1997, a plan was presented for the implementation of computerized risk analysis and new work methods. This National Risk Analysis Program involves the use of risk assessment in all aspects of customs work. The program is aimed at: (i) introducing the use of risk analysis; (ii) improving service to the legal trade; and (iii) allocating resources to areas of "high" risk.

The risk analysis system includes:

- a computerized customs clearance system;
- an automatic control system;
- a flexible profiling system with national and local profile facilities;
- an automatic, paperless results and feedback system;
- a follow-up system with detailed error and results management and statistics, as well as a management

information tool to aid in planning and management;

- a random control system which selects a few low-risk entries for manual control (red route) to verify the quality of risk assessment and to detect new error trends;
- a historical database with all the information from customs declarations, to provide a proper tool for risk assessment in the initial control and post control stages;
- a data warehousing system to allow risk analysis specialists to make risk assessments based on errors from the profiling system and on strategic information from the historical database; and
- an electronic communication and information system (Internet, Intranet, and E-mail) for risk analysis specialists.

A new concept is also now being explored and developed as part of a nationwide cooperation program involving customs, the government, and economic circles. This concept takes the experience gathered from the risk analysis program a step further. A "stairway" of facilities would be offered to economic operators who undertake to assume more active and professional roles in customs procedures.

The Stairway

Through risk assessment and quality assurance of customs procedures, the stairway approach aims to match the level of customs services and facilities to the level and quality of input provided by economic operators. The objective is to improve the quality of customs performance and to simplify and rationalize customs procedures. The stairway approach is based on a number of principles:

- comprehensiveness—all foreign trade should be included;
- beneficial effects of participating in the effort;

- optional level of service and benefits to individual companies; and
- better, higher-quality service and simpler customs procedures.

Thus, additional efforts made by an individual company, in cooperation with customs, would be rewarded. At the same time, customs administrations would achieve greater rationalization. The intent is for customs as well as economic operators to benefit from the approach.

Figure 5.1 shows the various steps on the stairway. Steps 1 and 2 on the stairway are based on the traditional customs controls (physical examination, documentation, audit, random control, etc.). In steps 3 and 4, the individual company will carry out these types of controls as agreed with customs. The latter will then administer the process and check the quality of, for example, an import declaration according to conditions in the agreement. The exercise of customs authority in the future will depend on which step the individual company has reached on the stairway. By being on steps 3 and 4, a company can avoid undesired interruption in the flow of goods.

The Stairway

OPPORTUNITIES	REQUIREMENTS
– Certificate of quality – Automatic clearance – No interruption in flow of goods, etc.	– ISO-certification – Quality Random Control (QRC)
– Periodical declaration – Priority compliance, etc.	– Quality of all customs routines
----- *"Quality approved" company* -------	----- *"Quality approved" company* -------
– Approved importer – Limited automatic clearance, etc.	– Quality of some Custom routines – EDI-permission
– Import/export and transit	– Declaration of acceptance quality
----- *"Reliable" company* -----	----- *"Reliable" company* -------------

To derive maximum benefit from the anticipated change, Swedish Customs is introducing a new organization with the following basic features:

- one authority, one Swedish Customs;
- process orientation;
- the same resources but more officials in operational roles;
- a new central organization for strategic management; and
- six new customs regions.

The new Swedish Customs will push vigorously for simplified rules and procedures in accordance with the Stockholm declaration. It will prepare for and carry out its responsibility for Sweden's chairmanship of EU 2001. With its new organization, it expects to coordinate international matters more capably and contribute actively to various development projects in the customs field.

6

Risk Analysis: A New Tool for Customs Efficiency and Enforcement

Rafael Arana

The objectives of risk analysis are to bring greater returns in enforcement, and to reach maximum administrative effectiveness. Preventive risk analysis is necessary to ensure rapid and efficient customs procedures such as:

- control of ships and other means of transport;
- container control within customs facilities;
- control of expeditions to free areas and deposits;
- transit control; and
- control of customs clearances.

For risk analysis, it is necessary to define the risk and to evaluate it. Risk evaluation affects customs procedures, and vice versa, as shown below:

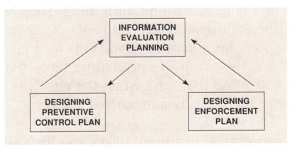

Note: Many details of implementation are not suitable for publication and are not included in these pages.

Risk analysis needs information. The customs offices, especially the customs headquarters, are responsible for gathering the information needed. Both internal and external information has to be obtained automatically, without affecting the smooth flow of procedures or disrupting the day-to-day operation of the office. Risk analysis should not be a reason for delays and should not interfere with customs procedures. Preventive risk analysis has to be efficient to make efficient automation and computerization possible.

The evaluation and planning of risk analysis has two phases. The first one, the design of the preventive control plan, deals with clearance of goods (e.g., using an automated system with filters) and detection of customs infringements (e.g., using programmed container control). The second phase is the design of the enforcement plan—how the details of the first plan are to be implemented.

The analysis of import consignments uses a "filter" program which, on the basis of various criteria (operator, tariff heading, origin, value, etc.), classifies consignments into one of three channels: green (automatic passage), orange (document check), or red (physical check). These filters facilitate the dispatch of goods.

There are two types of filters: objective and subjective filters. Objective filters are established by the Department of Customs and Excise Duties to conform to legal measures or central criteria. They are generally applicable and cannot be amended by the local customs authorities. Subjective filters are established at the local level and apply only to the office where they have been developed and only for a limited time. There are also two levels of uncertainty: those that go with the filter and those that arise when the circuit is modified. The shape of the filters is summarized below:

Description: general definition of the specific filter.
Circuit: green, orange, or red, indicating the rate established for the color.

Orders: in the form of digits of two figures or a figure and a letter, indicative of the measures to be taken by the customs officer for declarations affected by the filter.

Date of Entry: day, month, and year in which the filter was created.

Date of Consolidation: day, month, and year of acceptance of the filter by the system. Normally, it corresponds to the date of entry.

Date of Expiration: day, month, and year in which the filter will cease to be valid.

Parameters (export)
- statistical position
- country of destination
- customs procedure
- exporter
- declarant
- statistical value

Parameters (import)
- statistical position
- country of origin
- tariff preferences
- tariff reduction
- customs procedure
- importer
- declarant
- statistical value

Spain's Central Department has so far created 78 filters for exports and 308 for imports.

The filters' level of access works as follows. First, documents are assigned to customs officers through a filter program. The officers enter the details into the system, which has two levels of access: first, the local director, and second, the customs officers. The first level is responsible for the following tasks: checking objective and subjective filters, determining the need for additional subjective filters, and ensuring randomness control. The second level is responsible only for checking objective and subjective filters for a particular consignment.

The filter system includes special procedures. Rapid withdrawal of goods is not explicitly provided for in the system, but decisions in this regard can be made on the basis of risk parameters. Previous import declarations are partially implemented in the system, but can be rejected according to risk parameters. Customs clearance on operators' premises is integrated in the system. Subjective filters are applied with great effectiveness.

To maintain, update, and improve the filter system, a special working group at the customs central headquarters performs scheduled and specific updates of the system, progressively transforming the subjective filters into objective filters as the system improvement plan is implemented.

The Customs Infringements Detection Plan, a new program which deals with containers, has been considered as a model by the "Fight Against Fraud in Containers" seminar in Paris. Its objective is to follow up specific containers and the preparation of container profiles, which may not necessarily be consistent with the goods. The program derives its information from computerized summary declarations as shown below:

- The declarant must send the data on the declarations through teleprocessing.
- The electronic message will include all the data on the paper declaration, that is to say, a complete image of the declaration. Compulsorily, for each declaration, information about the commercial invoice with its number will be included as well as the name of the transport and other additional documents that may be required. Missing requirements will cause the rejection of the declaration and, therefore, nonadmission.
- The inclusion in the message of a reference to a certain

document means that the document is in the hands of the declarant.

- Customs has the option to set the final time of transfer of documents for the day.
- Coherence verification:
    - rejection of Single Administrative Document (SAD) that do not comply with computer validation;
    - numbering of valid declarations;
    - allocation of admitted declarations to the red or orange circuit; and
    - provisional allocation of the rest of the admitted declarations to green.
- A reply is transmitted to the declarant specifying:
    - rejected documents and the reason for rejection;
    - numbers of declarations that have been assigned provisionally to the green circuit. Customs may change the allocations to the red or orange circuits within a few hours. No action from customs within a given period will imply confirmation of the green circuit and, therefore, automatic release of the merchandise.
- An automatic clearance message is sent to the declarant.

Operators transmit data to the respective seaport authorities who send the data online to the customs authority. Other programs, mainly in the enforcement area, complement the analysis, making it possible to check containers that are already suspect. Besides five peripheral units of analysis in the ports of Barcelona, Valencia, Bilbao, Algeciras, and Las Palmas, a Container Control Center, based in Madrid, handles the following tasks:

- coordination of peripheral units;
- establishment of risk profiles;
- management of the Sea Info system;

- follow-up of containers under alert; and
- exchange of information with other countries.

The computerized container system is centralized for online consultation. It includes several databases on tax-payers, excise tax, imports, exports, transit, and summary declarations. Different applications link all the databases.

The Summary Declaration computer program is another new initiative. It controls all merchandise at customs premises. Electronic data transfer allows customs officers to obtain online information regarding a specific summary declaration. Customs staff can thus make use of the experience of their colleagues to improve the efficiency of their own procedures. The search for specific summary declarations is assigned priority in accordance with factors such as the status of the declaration. A risk analysis application within the Summary Declaration program applies risk profiles to consignments. This work is done either before or at the same time as the normal (filter) customs clearance process.

As stated above, the program allows customs authorities to search for summary declarations according to one or more criteria. The result of the search is then shown in a summary declaration, which contains the following information:

- number of the summary declaration;
- status;
- date of presentation of the summary declaration;
- responsibility for transportation;
- number of consignments;
- means of transport;
- port of destination of the means of transport;
- regular/nonregular line; and
- simplified procedure applied.

Specific container search or selection is possible. The search criteria are: the customs office, the date, and the container identification code. Once the container is selected, the following information is available: container details, consignments, summary declaration, and customs declaration.

Risk analysis of consignments permits selection of consignments with given risk profiles. Various criteria can be combined:

- customs office;
- origin of the goods;
- country and port where goods are loaded;
- tariff heading;
- weight;
- number of bulks; and
- risk index (for smuggling of tobacco and drugs).

Through different screens the following information is obtained:

- number of the summary declaration;
- consignment number;
- status of the summary declaration;
- date of admission of the summary declaration;
- means of transport;
- origin of the goods;
- point of loading;
- destination;
- tariff heading;
- number of bulks;
- weight;
- risk index for tobacco and drugs;
- transport representative;
- number of the container;
- description of the goods;
- clearance declaration; and
- location within the customs area.

The program automatically allocates a risk index for cigarettes and drugs (from 0 to 3). The calculation is based on the information and profiles previously established, taking into account various criteria such as origin and type of goods. The customs officer may decide to investigate only beyond a minimum risk index.

The Container Control Center, fed with data from specific sources, can keep track of suspicious containers. Summary Declarations entering the system are cross-checked against the list of "risky" containers.

Through the system described above and the application of risk analysis, enforcement activity yields greater returns while facilitating trade for the vast majority of transactions.

7

The Role of Information Technology in Customs Modernization

Buenaventura Maniego

Introduction

This paper relates the experience of the Philippine Bureau of Customs with information technology, particularly with a computerization and modernization program that has been touted as "the gateway to efficiency in customs processes."

Some Philippine customs employees used to be awed by computers and were afraid of computerization. They were apprehensive about touching the keyboards, afraid of making mistakes. Yet they went ahead and conquered their fears. Now these very same people have quickly learned how to work with computers. Now, they manipulate computers and check customs documentation quickly and with ease.

Computerization in the Bureau, as in the rest of the Philippines, did not happen overnight. It took us several years to arrive where we are now. Way back in the late 1970s we first attempted to use electronic data processing. But when the gigantic computer broke down in the late 1970s, that was the end of computerization for us at the time.

The first serious attempt to computerize the Bureau took place in the late 1990s when Guillermo L. Parayno Jr. took over as Commissioner. He instituted reforms and strengthened systems and technology use in the Bureau. Our computerization and modernization program, he said, was our "quantum leap into the future."

Milestones

To implement the computerization program, as part of the broader Philippine Tax Computerization Program, Unisys Philippines was contracted to integrate the ASYCUDA++ (Automated System for Customs Data Management) software developed by the United Nations Conference on Trade and Development (UNCTAD) with the Bureau's computer-based activities. ASYCUDA++, a computerized application system that conforms to international codes and standards, is used in more than 65 countries worldwide.

In 1995, ASYCUDA++ was adapted to Philippine requirements. The result was the Automated Customs Operations Systems (ACOS). The introduction of ACOS in the Bureau and the use of information technology in providing service to the trade community have helped facilitate the flow of cargo.

Starting in 1996, and at a hectic pace, we introduced electronic lodgement facilities, including the following:

- *Entry Encoding System.* Importers/brokers in all major ports in the Philippines can now have their import entry declaration documents digitized at this service center, which is managed by the Philippine Chamber of Commerce and Industry.
- *Direct Traders Input.* This is one of the first remote electronic lodgement facilities. Importers and brokers can lodge their entries from their offices using a dial-up facility.
- *Data Warehouse System.* This was installed in 1997, pushing the Bureau to the forefront of information technology use. The system provides timely and accurate trade information on trade balances and trends.

It has since been enhanced by a user application system, the *Customs Decision Support System (CDSS)*, which has become the knowledge base for post-audit, economic intelligence, and other customs processes.

- *Customs Web Site*. This was developed and installed in 1998 and is being enhanced this year.
- *Electronic Data Interchange*. Launched in June 1998, this has made possible the electronic lodgement of warehousing entries.

All the information technology initiatives of the Bureau have been integrated under its computerization and modernization program.

Main Systems Modules

Electronic inward manifest

Shipping lines and airlines submit to the Bureau all cargo manifests in electronic format through the worldwide facilities of the Société Internationale de Télécommunications Aéronautiques, as well as through the Consolidators Data Exchange Centre.

Electronic lodgement of import entries

Importers use the Entry Encoding Centers (EECs) at the customs houses which are operated by a private entity, the Philippine Chamber of Commerce and Industry. The paper declarations are digitized in the EECs so that they can be electronically processed in ACOS.

For paperless transactions, the Bureau's first major effort is the Direct Traders Input facility, or DTI. Importers or brokers key in data on their import entries into their office computers using a set format. The data are lodged remotely in the Bureau's computer system. The use of the DTI facility has cut processing time. It used to take several days to clear shipments from customs; now it takes only a few hours.

The Bureau has also implemented the use of Electronic Data Interchange (EDI) in ACOS. The system offers a full range of communications and messengering protocols and data transmission options.

The EDI Gateway System provides UN EDIFACT vans with translation capability. Web-page forms are provided by the General Electric Information System (GEIS).

ACOS SELECTIVITY System

The implementation of ACOS drastically changed the clearing of shipments through customs. At the heart of ACOS is a computer program called SELECTIVITY. It is an intelligent system that analyzes the risk profiles of shipments. It does this by comparing the shipments' particulars with about 18 reference files or screens, and then categorizing the shipments into high-, medium-, and low-risk transactions.

SELECTIVITY in ACOS enables the Bureau to focus its limited enforcement resources on a more manageable number of shipments, thus making customs intervention more intelligent and effective. The automated assessment in ACOS, on the other hand, improves revenue generation by ensuring the consistent and accurate application of tax rules and the availability of updated reference tables and files. By the way, the Philippine customs service collects 25 percent to 30 percent of the total revenue intake of the government.

Data Warehouse System

SGS developed and implemented the Data Warehouse System of the Bureau. The application has revolutionized the way in which the Bureau defines, analyzes, and accesses trade data. The Data Warehouse System is, as the name implies, a dedicated storage facility for information during the processing of transactions. The Data Warehouse uses import transaction data from SGS CRFs, ACOS, the Bureau's Valuation and Classification Library, and other external sources.

The information is used for a number of customs purposes (e.g., valuation, audit, intelligence, trade statistics). It can also be made available to the public once it has been suitably edited to prevent breaches of security and commercial confidentiality.

The Data Warehouse System does not only provide easy access to relevant and trade data and statistics, but, most importantly, it builds a knowledge base for the future.

The Bureau's Assessment Division, Intelligence Enforcement Group, and the office of the Commissioner can access the Data Warehouse through the Customs Decision Support System (CDSS) application.

To summarize, these are the dramatic changes brought about by computerization in the Philippine Bureau of Customs.

	Before Computerization	After Computerization
Required signatures	79	5
Cargo release time	6–8 days	4 to 6 hours for green lane 48 hours for yellow and red lanes
Shipments examined	All	15% physical examination (red) 15% document examination (yellow) 70% no examination (green)
Supporting documents required	Payment orders, official receipts, and proof of bank payments	Payments are made to banks and electronically transmitted to Bureau of Customs by computer
Place of examination	Anywhere in the port	Designated examination areas
Accountable forms required	Many forms	Single Administrative Document (SAD)
Inward manifest documents submitted to Bureau	13	3 copies in electronic format

Partnerships with the Private Sector

Large organizations, such as the Philippine Chamber of Commerce and Industry, Philippine Federation of Industries, Port Users' Confederation, and Chamber of Customs Brokers, Inc., have observed the following advantages resulting from the computerization of the Bureau:

- faster release of cargoes (selectivity; imports delivered more quickly to manufacturers/industrialists; paperless; queueless; cashless);
- lower customs cost (hassle-free; less contact with customs);
- reduced pilferage (faster turnover; less time for pilferage); and
- less corruption at the pier (much red tape has been eliminated; paper processing has been reduced to a minimum).

All of these benefits gained in the computerization program are the result of the partnership between the Bureau of Customs and the private sector, including, among others, the following:

- Philippine Chamber of Commerce and Industry;
- SGS;
- UNCTAD;
- Unisys;
- Asian Terminal Incorporated;
- International Container Terminal Services, Inc.;
- Port Users' Confederation;
- Chamber of Customs Brokers, Inc.; and
- Brokers and Importers Data Access.

Conclusion

The government and the private sector share the following vision:

A customs service more responsive to clients' needs and supportive of government goals, adhering to the world's best practices—a customs service that all Filipinos can be truly proud of.

Compared with other customs administrations not only in the Asia-Pacific but also in other member countries of the World Customs Organization (most of which have over 20 years of experience in the use of information technology), the Philippine Bureau of Customs' use of information technology is in its infancy. But during the last three years and especially in 1998, the Bureau finally went down the road that other countries have traveled for many years. The Philippines is ready to learn and willing to do its part in extending the boundaries of knowledge in the field of electronic governance.

The success of its computerization program has earned for the Bureau of Customs praise and recognition from local and foreign organizations including the WCO, the UN, the IMF, and foreign visitors from all over the world.

A UN report stated:

The Review team was greatly impressed with the progress achieved in modernizing the cargo clearance operations. In a very short time, new systems and procedures implemented have significantly improved revenue collection, considerably speeded up the clearance of cargo and led to a marked improvement in staff morale and image.

Another report by the UNCTAD Audit Team said that,

Among the developing countries, you rank no. 1 in computerization. Industrialized countries which had 20 to 25 years' experience did not accomplish what you achieved in so short a time.

Unquestionably these international accolades heaped on the Bureau and the compliments from people who have dealt with the Bureau for many years have bolstered the agency's morale. But the journey is not yet over. We still have to improve some systems and programs as part of our modernization.

Our biggest dream now and our deepest concern is to become not only a world-class customs service but also a world leader in electronic governance.

8

Relations Between Customs and Private Operators in Finland

Leo Nissinen

New Role of Customs in International Trade

Formalities, procedures, and paperwork in international trade arise from the need for both governments and trade operators to monitor and control the movement of goods and the transfer of services, and to safeguard the legitimate interests of all parties. Over the years, trade facilitation efforts made by international or national bodies in various sectors (e.g., the World Customs Organization and the European Commission) have improved trade-related information flows by simplifying and harmonizing the procedures and the documentation, and standardizing commercial practices. Without cooperation between customs and the business sector, trade facilitation efforts cannot succeed.

The systems developed to link shippers, transport operators, port authorities, bankers, insurance companies, customs, consignees, and others in the business of international trade are constantly being adapted to meet changing needs associated in particular with the speed of modern transport, express freight deliveries, and containerization. Today, information flows are at a point between paper documents still often painfully filled out by hand, those produced by computer but still sent manually over the Internet, and other automatic data transmission possibilities. The solution to customs logistics problems with the business sector is to use simplified customs procedures combined with EDI customs clearance systems.

Relations with the Trade Community in Finland

In Finland, good cooperation with traders consists of the following elements:

- customs' client strategy;
- customer orientation in customs work;
- organizations for cooperation with the trade community;
- tailor-made customs procedures;
- ADP cooperation with EDI customs clearance system; and
- customer information and training.

The strategies and objectives are summarized in below:

Strategies and Objectives of Trade Relations in Finland

Level	Target-Centered	Customer Orientation	Management
National	–Risk analysis model –Resources model	–Model of customer-related simplified procedures	–Central values –Management methods
District	–District-related application and allocation	–Coverage of consulting –Coverage of tailored procedures	–Process management –Values adoption
Office	–Assignment and results	–Customer management and customer feedback	–Progress of authorization –Process control
Individual	–Multiple skills –Competence	–Multiple skills –Competence	–Discussions –Commitment –Team work

Customs' client orientation

The main goal of the strategy is the smooth flow of foreign trade. Clients fall into three categories:

- Group A – registered contracting customers;
- Group B – average customers; and
- Group C – risk customers.

Customers in group A apply tailor-made, simplified, computerized customs procedures; their customs clearances are accurate, and their securities in proper order. Risk customers are always submitted to stricter control: the logistics of the customs clearance process are more complicated (no simplifications, stricter control of documents and goods, higher securities). The control of registered contracting customers (group A) consists only in tax audits and spot-checks on goods.

Organizations for cooperation between Finnish Customs and traders

A variety of organizations exist to foster public/private cooperation in customs:

- Customs-Trade Consultative Committee. The main goal of this cooperation group is to improve cooperation and understanding between customs and the business sector. Among its members are:
  - Director-General of the Finnish Customs and some other directors;
  - Central Chamber of Commerce of Finland;
  - Federation of Finnish Commerce and Trade;
  - Confederation of Finnish Industry and Employers;
  - Federation of Finnish Enterprises;
  - Finnish Freight Forwarders Association;

- Finnish Trucking Association; and
- Finnish Shipowners Association.
- Customs Clearance and IT Cooperation Group. This group gives guidance in the use of customs procedures, especially simplified procedures, and in the electronic transmission of customs clearance information to customs through EDI (Edifact messages) or magnetic disks. Its members are the Board of Customs, forwarding agents, and major Finnish companies in industry and wholesale trade.
- Sea Traffic Customer Cooperation Group.
- Customs Cooperation Group concerning Logistics and Trade with Russia.
- Ad hoc group meetings with industry, trade, or forwarding agents concerning customs procedures and IT questions, etc.

Tailor-made customs procedures

Procedures are tailored to three categories of registered customers:

- industrial enterprises, i.e., "bulk model" (raw oil, chemicals, ore, scrap metal, raw wood), and "factory model" (electronics, machinery parts, etc.);
- wholesale enterprises, i.e., "wholesale model" (technological goods, investment goods), and "central-company model" (all kinds of consumer goods); and
- forwarding agents, i.e., "forwarding agents model" (all kinds of goods and customers) and courier transport enterprises (express freight goods).

In addition, cash customers include both enterprises and natural persons, and service processes for minor customers.

Conclusion

Customs plays a key role in international trade. It is clear that the manner in which customs conducts its business has a substantial impact on the movement of goods across international borders. On the other hand, if traders expect greater facilitation of import and export procedures by customs, then they themselves must be willing to contribute to the building of an environment of trust and cooperation which will enable that facilitation to become a reality.

III: The Airline Industry: A Case Study

9

Customs Simplification: An International Airline Perspective

Geoffrey Barrington

Introduction

The name of British Airways World Cargo is familiar to many. According to the last annual industry statistics, British Airways World Cargo is the fifth largest scheduled carrier of air cargo in the world, an achievement of which we are especially proud, given the fact that British Airways only operates with passenger-carrying aircraft.

How do we achieve it? The main reasons, among others, are:

- We manage our capacity very closely.
- We supplement our capacity with key partnerships where necessary to meet our customers' demands through our global route network, which is our key resource.

These demands also require us to listen to our customers and to support them in partnership. We recognize the importance of our role in the global supply chain.

Background

In the early 1990s, we realized that we had to make significant changes in the way that we did business if we were to realize the increasing opportunities that would be available in the future. This realization became a vision, and we have spent the last three years turning that vision into a reality. At the top of the agenda was a major capital investment of US$400 million in a new hub facility in London to handle over 800,000 tonnes a year. This investment has not been restricted to London. We have also invested across our entire global network to ensure that all our freight and documents are bar-coded, and we have established EDI links for all our customers. We are also building a new 90,000-sq. ft. temperature-controlled fresh-produce complex in London to handle 100,000 tonnes of perishable produce. This will double our capacity and current revenues of US$72 million a year.

Our vision was not just about facilities, it was about people and cultures, together with a change in the way we did business and in the processes and procedures we had relied upon for several decades. Make no mistake: change is never easy and in a large organization it presents major challenges. As a business we had to rise to the challenges. Our shareholders demanded it, our customers required it, and, equally as important, our staff wanted it. We invested over 100,000 man-hours in training our staff over the last six months of 1998 alone. We have made the transition and are now starting to realize the benefits.

The sheer scope and speed of these changes are realities of the modern business climate and in some way, we feel, illustrate the increasing pressures on trade facilitation. This is not to suggest that the extent of the change in customs administrations and their procedures needs to be as great. We realize that the speed of change will always be faster in the modern business environment than in regulatory and control regimes.

However, given the speed of change, it would not be unrealistic to believe that customs procedures in ten years' time will be totally different from those of today and very much more streamlined. But beware: our business requirements will also have changed by that time. It is a step-change program that is already accelerating.

As a scheduled operator, we do, of course, have our own difficulties when moving our consumables, aircraft spares, and support equipment around the globe. We are also very aware of the complexities and differences in customs procedures. As a carrier primarily we are not directly involved with commercial cargo clearance and other inward-processing regimes. However, we do move goods under bond and operate customs-bonded warehouses. Furthermore, as carrier we are held liable under many customs procedures, especially in the event of inadvertent discrepancies. These discrepancies cost us real money.

It is not my intention to discuss the reasons behind the accelerating growth in world trade, other than to say that deregulation has positively encouraged air transportation and expanded it into new areas, not least of which is new entrants into the market. Despite deregulation, the industry still remains beset by regulatory control, often in the name of "consumer interests" or "consumer protection."

The growth in the trade of goods, however, is increasingly determined by the efficiency of customs processes. We should not forget the two fundamental roles of customs: revenue collection and protection of society.

In an address to the UNCTAD World Automated Systems for Customs Data Management (ASCYCUDA) meeting in Manila in the spring of 1998, the Secretary General of WCO referred to the balancing act of today's customs administrations, among "competing interests of revenue collection, trade facilitation, enforcement of trade instruments and the increasing demands for social and environmental protection."

The reduction or outright removal of trade barriers has

turned more of the focus onto protecting society. In international trade we recognize that protection does take account of other interests, such as cultural differences and the need for protection against transnational crime, especially the traffic in drugs, counterfeit goods, endangered species, nuclear and biological material, and money laundering. This protection, however, must not be seen as substituting one form of control for another, as it would further complicate and break up trade patterns and flows. The WCO has some 150 member states, nearly all of which have different sets of customs procedures. This in itself is a clear demonstration of the need for harmonization.

The current deficiencies of customs are the following:

- their interventionist nature;
- reliance on transaction-based controls;
- lack of transparency of procedures;
- issues of corruption and integrity;
- little or no redress for error;
- inadequate resources;
- low level of training;
- lack of cooperation; and
- outdated technology or even a total lack of automation.

The scene seems bleak worldwide, but increasingly we are becoming aware of customs administrations that are addressing these deficiencies. Through seminars such as the ASEM Seminar in February 1999 at the Asian Development Bank in Manila we hope to use our influence for change. It is not our intention to tell people how to do things, but to support them and to cooperate in reaching common goals.

The Way Forward

Customs integrity. We look forward to the implementation of the 1993 WCO Declaration—Arusha Guidelines, which include simple, consistent, transparent customs procedures.

Customs efficiency. To operate efficiently, customs administrations worldwide will likewise require:

- modern legislation;
- service-based culture and service-level standards; and
- streamlined organization.

Accession to international instruments. More countries should accede to the instruments that have been developed internationally to simplify and harmonize customs transactions, such as those of the WCO:

- Harmonized Code System;
- Valuation Agreement;
- Nairobi Convention;
- Rules of Origin; and
- Kyoto Convention.

In fact, we should consider mandating WTO signatories to accede to the Kyoto Convention and to set aside any reservations and variations they may have.

Convergence of controls. This can be achieved through:

- seamless intervention by a single control agency;
- increased investment in modern technology for inspection and detection equipment;
- automation and eventual adoption of electronic data interchange
  - separate physical and fiscal controls,
  - paperless processing of air cargo transactions,

- standard data elements using standard data formats to enable
  - pre-arrival processing and release, and
  - post-entry clearance,
- risk management and selectivity programs for profiling and intelligence to develop inspection based on risk analysis,
- audit-based control, and
- accession to and implementation of the Montreal Protocol 4;
- new alliances between the public and private sectors through MOU and tripartite programs; and
- coordinated efforts on a national, regional, and global basis.

It would be remiss in this short presentation to overlook two very encouraging developments:

- the G7 initiative to simplify and harmonize customs procedures; and
- the international trade prototype being developed between the USA and the UK.

Consultation

With our global hub operation based in London, it is essential to our business that we work as closely as possible with our own customs administration, as indeed we would with any other administration, as necessary. The result has been our ability to develop short-term solutions that facilitate our operations and to establish practical guidelines on new procedures necessary in an ever-developing business.

The UK has placed much emphasis on consultation, and UK Customs has an established and successful Joint Customs Consultative Committee that brings together customs and trade on a regular basis. Let me say from personal experience that this committee does not always produce a consensus of opinion, but it has given all parties a fair opportunity to cooperate and to discuss issues in a genuine consultative forum.

Of major impact to the interests of both UK Customs and British Airways has been the success of the MOU on illegal drug control. The MOU has support from the very top of both organizations and is regularly reviewed by senior managers from Customs and BA. It has not changed the "law" but it has greatly facilitated our interface with Customs. The success of the MOU and the further development of the tripartite MOU agreements that are now being signed must not be understated.

As an international operator we are no strangers to the need for consultation and lobbying. Where possible, we work through industry associations at the national, regional, and international levels. We are active members of regional associations such as the AEA. Its EC Working Group in particular enables us to respond regularly to and work with the EC, in such activities as the current search for real solutions to the issues of transit reform in Europe. Globally, we are proactive within IATA, particularly its Cargo Facilitation Panel, which is currently developing air consignment guidelines.

Before closing, may I highlight a growing concern. There are too many overlapping bodies and organizations (WTO, UNECE, UNCTAD, UNCITRAL, IMO, ICAO, EC, APEC, NAFTA, ASEAN, WCO, OECD, IMF, and World Bank, to name a few) seemingly striving to be flag-bearers of facilitation and equally as many trade associations wanting to be heard.

Conclusion

Let me conclude by raising the stakes a little higher. A key reason for the growth in procedural obstacles is "the lack of political will among governments to seek comprehensive solutions or to place simplification of procedures sufficiently high on their domestic or international trade agendas."[1] This statement does not come from the private sector but from the European Commission itself.

As a leading international carrier we are proud of having provided customs with the highest standards of assistance and cooperation, but we must now seek to ensure that real facilitation prizes go to the best compliance performers.

Trade will continue to grow, and the proportion carried by air is set to increase. Unless there is a coherent plan to modernize customs procedures worldwide, we must look at customs as inhibiting this growth. As an international carrier we are not willing to stand aside and let this happen, and will seek to take whatever action is appropriate to influence change. Individually we cannot influence the future growth in trade between Europe and Asia, but collectively we can facilitate the future. We must therefore examine every opportunity to simplify and harmonize procedures.

The demands are growing. We must move forward with firm resolve. We can form a partnership and that process must begin right now. Real facilitation is not a question of gains and concessions but the achievement of gains for all concerned. The fact that an estimated 2–10 percent of product costs are attributable to customs and other control regimes suggests that there is a multibillion-dollar reason for change.

For British Airways World Cargo real facilitation across our global business could increase our contribution to the profitability of British Airways by an estimated US$120 million yearly. We are constantly challenged by change, and, like many others in our sector, we are only too willing to share with customs administrations the lessons and experience of such change. After all, we all have a very real interest in the outcome.

---

[1] "Assessment of the Scope for WTO Rules in the Field of Import, Export and Customs Procedures," EC DGI Document G/C/W/112, 22 September 1998.

10

The Integrated Air Express Industry

James Goh

This paper presents the views of the Conference of Asia Pacific Express Carriers (CAPEC) on:

- the integrated air express industry and its development;
- customers of the integrated air express industry and their expectations in today's global market;
- risk management—the challenges and perspective of the integrated air express industry;
- customs administrations and the integrated air express industry
    - their role in today's global market,
    - shared responsibility and the importance of "strategic partnership," and
    - convergence of objectives—balancing enforcement and facilitation;
- change management—the mind-set of customs administrations and the integrated air express industry; and
- the way forward—economic growth and the goals of trade liberalization and trade facilitation.

There is an important element of shared responsibility between customs administrations and the integrated air express industry. Strategic partnership, cooperation, consultation, and sharing of experiences and expertise between customs administrations and the industry can help achieve and increase trade efficiency and community protection. Businesses can thus be helped to succeed and, ultimately, economies to prosper. However, in order for us to achieve this collectively, there must be change, just as the economic makeup of the world has changed over the past few years.

It has become commonplace to talk about change in the world today. Who would have predicted an economic crisis in Asia a few years ago? As the world economy continues to progress, change is inevitable. The language of economics today is the language of change and the language of the transnational corporations, of companies with global operations but a local perspective in each country. The ongoing change due to economic growth and development will affect customs administrations and the integrated air express industry and will continue to do so, a reality which some of the sunset industries still have not come to grips with.

The Integrated Air Express Industry

For those who are not familiar with the integrated air express industry, a brief history may be interesting. From its humble origin in the late 1960s as the international air courier industry, the integrated air express business has evolved into competing with the traditional airfreight forwarders and, in some countries, even directly with the local postal authorities. Integrated air express carriers, unlike the traditional airfreight forwarders, offer door-to-door pickup and delivery, cross-border transportation, customs clearance, and delivery service to the entire spectrum of the commercial world and for almost any commodity.

Because speed, reliability, and value-added service are the hallmarks of an integrated air express carrier, there are size and value restrictions which vary from country to country. But generally, the integrated air express industry deals with the business requirements of the global market and its economic changes, within the permissible limits of regulatory provisions, especially those of customs. The bulk of what we carry is still lightweight, a mix of documents and low-value merchandise. However, with the rapid change in the global market and with economic development, we are beginning to see that size, value, and commodity have also changed to reflect heavier weights with higher value.

How large the market for cross-border integrated air express business is, is anybody's guess. However, the combined revenue of the four founding members of CAPEC alone was in excess of US$60 billion in 1998—300 million in units handled and 1.5 million tons in volume. And annual growth, in volume terms, is 20–45 percent, varying from country to country, a staggering quantity as far as customs is concerned.

The integrated air express business today is at takeoff time. The world has become smaller. Time and management techniques have become a key competitive edge for global customers. Delivery information has become as important as the delivery of the goods itself. Players in the industry are grappling with the challenge to provide product homogeneity and service flexibility across national and cultural boundaries. And the traditional segregation of the air transport industry between postal, air courier, and airfreight forwarders has lost its relevance. For example, components manufactured in one country today may be assembled into finished goods in a second country and then distributed to many markets worldwide.

For the past 30 years, the development of the integrated air express business was constrained by:

- poor communications infrastructure;
- visible and invisible barriers to trade;
- inability of customs to accept and manage change and quickly adapt procedures to keep up with economic change and technological development; and
- lack of understanding of the integrated air express business.

The results were:

- frequent, time-consuming, and costly delays at customs and ports of entry (for example, consignments could lie in customs longer than it took to transport them from one country to another);
- high demurrage charges; and
- costly downtime if plans were late, tenders missed deadlines, or replacement parts were not available.

An extremely important point which must be emphasized is that all the above extra charges will be passed on to the businesses, which means that the cost of doing business will increase, thereby affecting not only a nation's economic competitiveness but also its foreign investments.

The main problems were costly global telecommunications and customs administrations that were restrictive, enforcement-minded, and revenue-focused rather than dedicated to global trade facilitation. These obstacles forced integrated air express carriers to develop more costly ways to achieve their business objectives and, of course, these extra costs were passed on to clients, thereby increasing their cost of doing business.

But now is a time of change for both customs and the integrated air express industry. It is a time when the combined pressures of the global marketplace, of customers, of less government intervention in business, and of global economic growth and development are bringing us closer together and with increasingly aligned objectives. Today, customs and the integrated air express industry could not be in a better position to act for their mutual benefit and for the ultimate mutual benefit of our global customers.

Customers of the Integrated Air Express Industry

The customers of the integrated air express industry today expect door-to-door overnight service irrespective of the commodity or the value or weight of the consignment. This means:

- end-of-business-day collection;
- overnight transportation; and
- start-of-business-day or morning delivery.

The integrated air express industry is investing millions of dollars in a dedicated air transportation network to meet these customer expectations. All the companies already have comprehensive ground distribution infrastructure in place. The only missing link in many countries at the moment is the absence of pre-business hours customs clearance within 60 minutes of flight arrival, which would allow morning delivery to the global customers of today.

In keeping with the demands of the fast-changing global market, the integrated air express industry needs:

- pre-clearance of high- and low-value goods;
- release of low- and medium-value shipments directly from the consolidated shipping manifests of the integrated air express carriers;
- matching customs work-hours as and when the industry needs clearance;
- the same clearance treatment as postal shipments; and
- sixty minutes' customs clearance times upon flight arrival.

All that said, it must be emphasized strongly that global trade facilitation need not be at the expense of customs enforcement responsibilities. On the contrary, a strong strategic partnership between customs administrations and the integrated air express industry could further enhance enforcement.

Managing Risk

Effective risk management is as important to the integrated air express industry as it is to all customs administrations, and weighs very heavily in the international operations of the integrated air express industry, especially in the last couple of years. Just as customs administrations around the world are doing their best to manage risk effectively, the integrated air express industry is trying its very best to manage effectively the same set of risks.

I would like to highlight some of the challenges faced by the integrated air express industry in the management of risk. I sincerely hope that our common desire to manage risk more effectively will bring us closer together, with increasingly aligned objectives to help further our economic growth and development.

- *Training.* CAPEC member companies are spending a big chunk of our profits to train and upgrade the skills of our people. This is continuous, as we want our people to be highly trained and effective in meeting the challenges and changes of the new global market.
- *International operating procedures.* All our CAPEC member companies follow high-quality international operating procedures, very much aligned to world standards. We continue to keep ourselves updated to keep up with the demands of the new global market and the changes that have been forced upon us by rapid economic growth and development. We are very proud that all our CAPEC member companies are ISO-certified; some have even achieved international awards for their quality service.
- *Total control of the transportation cycle.* Many businesses

have been affected by the economic downturn in Asia. Most CAPEC member companies have nonetheless invested millions of dollars in a dedicated air transportation network to meet the demands of the new global market and the changes imposed by rapid economic growth and development. All CAPEC member companies already have comprehensive ground distribution infrastructure in place. While taking total control of the transportation cycle has many business objectives aligned to it, of paramount importance is minimizing risk.

- *Leveraging electronic commerce and the use of information technology.* Along with our investments in a dedicated air transportation network, all our CAPEC member companies are also investing millions of dollars in the development of information technology. The new global market, and its very rapid economic growth and development, presents us with tremendous opportunities for the use of technology in a number of important areas:
  - risk management, by providing good and reliable databases for risk analysis and targeting;
  - faster and possibly more effective global business processes;
  - efficient recordkeeping;
  - better service and reduced cost through automated operations; and
  - simplified and standardized international operations.

We have a unique opportunity to move forward with customs administrations in leveraging the use of technology for our common interest, just as we can develop a strategic partnership in the area of risk management.

Customs Administrations and the Integrated Air Express Industry

For customs administrations, it is a time when global and regional pressures are forcing a change in customs to facilitate rather than restrict trade. Technology is providing tremendous opportunities to speed up manual processes, to make more effective and timely use of information. While customs administrations differ, in general, developed customs administrations emphasize the following:

- streamlined movement of low-value, low-risk goods, including the adoption and implementation of the WCO guidelines for the handling of air-express shipments;
- facilitation (rather than intervention), using risk analysis and selective processing, and introducing amendments to legislation where necessary, in accordance with the annexes to the Kyoto Convention;
- reduced tariffs and licensing;
- greater reliance on consumption and other indirect taxes;
- use of GATT or WTO valuation code;
- increased use of customs automation and EDI for data collection and pre-clearance;
- simplified procedures, relying less on paper and requiring fewer signatures;
- support and man-dedicated air-express airport facilities;
- Memorandums of Understanding to build trust; and
- risk management.

These are but some of the trends noted in our work with both the WCO and customs administrations within APEC. In general, CAPEC hopes that all customs administrations will follow these trends. In making these suggestions, CAPEC is in no way belittling the need for customs to retain control at the border. Rather, we wish to assist customs in this undertaking by:

- reconciling our need for simplicity with customs need for information and regulatory integrity;
- recognizing the sophistication of smugglers and cooperating to help curb illicit activities;
- recognizing country imperatives and differences in the setting of customs' mission; and
- fostering close working relations with the WCO and its individual member customs administrations.

We have a unique opportunity to move forward with customs. In conclusion, this opportunity can be summed up as follows:

- Customs administrations and integrated air express carriers are closely linked.
- Both want to facilitate trade.
- Both are leveraging the use of technology.
- There is a unique opportunity to provide overnight delivery capability to support rapid economic growth, and customs and the integrated air express industry can play a substantial role in helping to make this happen.
- Customs and the integrated air express industry have shared risks and shared responsibility for managing risk.
- A forum is needed for CAPEC to interact with WCO and its member customs administrations to help facilitate change.

Together, we are in a position to take this strategic partnership a step further. Naturally, allowances would need to be made for country differences, but a regional charter for the integrated air express industry and customs could help enhance regional growth and economic interrelations for the common economic interest.

11

Air Cargo Facilitation

Robert Richardson

O n behalf of the 260 member air carriers of the International Air Transport Association (IATA), I would like to focus on a few critical issues of concern to the aviation community. For each of the points discussed below, the industry believes that there are reasonable solutions, many of which have already been implemented by forward-thinking states. In some instances, these solutions have required changes in national legislation. In others, the solutions have been the result of simple modifications in the way processes are carried out. However, in every case, the solutions have required a greater level of cooperation and trust between governments and the trade, as well as a shared vision of what changes were necessary and how they could best be implemented.

Introduction

Aviation carries but a small percentage of the total goods transported over international borders—only about 1 percent of movements (net value). That number might initially sound less than impressive and rather unimportant compared with the amount of goods carried by other modes of transportation. But it is the nature of the goods moved by air that makes our industry so vital to shippers, manufacturers, and even the states for which those goods are ultimately destined.

Compared with other modes of transport, such as shipping and rail, the air industry carries a significantly higher

99

percentage of high-value and time-critical consignments. Shippers, and their customers, depend on the speed inherent in aviation to meet the needs posed by just-in-time inventory controls, perishable-product movements, and critical-parts replacement, to name just a few.

Unfortunately, this benefit on which shippers and their customers depend for their economic well-being is often lost because of inefficient clearance of goods for release to home use. In too many cases today, in countries all around the globe, consignments arriving at their final destination take longer to be released from customs than the total time spent getting there.

This paper will also discuss the main rules and practices that govern the air transport sector. While these vary from state to state, they can be distilled down to their basic components for quick presentation. When moving goods, the air transport sector must:

- accept goods from shippers;
- document those goods;
- comply with import and export control regulations; and
- produce the goods at the destination with the necessary support documentation for entry, clearance, and release.

Each step of the process involves capturing specific data, creating paper documents for each consignment, creating other paper documents to reconcile the original documents, presenting the documents to customs authorities, and then archiving the documents for varying lengths of time after the goods have been moved. Needless to say, this is not an efficient or labor-friendly process. And it is made worse by the fact that a set of documents created for one phase in the process often does not satisfy the requirements of subsequent phases, resulting in the need for even more documents.

This process is repeated thousands of times each day, and is not limited only to movements by air. It is the same process relied upon by governments since the days of the sailing ships. It was slow and manpower-intensive then, and in today's environment of instant electronic communication and ever-shorter delivery deadlines, paper-based data exchange and inspection processes that do not rely upon risk assessment and selectivity criteria can bring the cargo industry to its knees.

The past 30 years have given rise to remarkable developments in the aviation industry, the business community, and in the way states view themselves and the world around them. The world has changed in so many ways. New opportunities are being discovered almost daily. Regrettably, however, the methods of moving goods across international borders have failed to keep pace. What has always been is not necessarily how things should be today, or in the future.

It is time that governments and the trade, with an eye to the needs of the future, undertake the necessary task of reviewing existing policies and practices and seek to implement new methods, using new technologies which will truly facilitate trade, while at the same time protecting national interests. Specifically, the air transport sector must act to realize the following achievable goals.

Paperless Transaction Processing

As described earlier, air carriers today must gather great quantities of data from shippers, often in electronic format, copy the data manually onto paper documents, attempt to verify their accuracy, and then transmit the information to the proper authorities. The authorities, on the other hand, often do the same thing in reverse. The entire process is plagued by unavoidable errors in data input, duplication of effort, waste of critical human resources for carrier and customs alike, and unnecessary costs for everyone.

A solution exists and its framework has been developed to realize the goal of making paperless transactions the norm instead of the exception. With the Montreal Protocol IV, we have an international convention that provides the legal basis for establishing electronic airway bills.

We in the industry recognize that such change will not come easily. We understand that many states will need to modify their national legislation to allow for exchange of electronic data. We also understand that many governments have yet to begin work on developing electronic data interchange (EDI) systems for cargo manifest processing.

Together, industry and government representatives have developed specific EDI programs, that is, computer-to-computer language formats and standardized messaging guidelines to reduce the time governments need to develop their capability in this critical area.

Many governments have made these choices, resulting, we believe, in significant cost reductions for themselves, the airlines, and the shippers, by making paper-based processes less inefficient. Manpower, so scarce in today's environment of shrinking budgets, has been redirected to productive activities such as enhanced customer service for the industry and strengthened enforcement by governments.

Harmonized Information Requirements

One of the most difficult and costly aspects of cargo movements is the lack of standardization in the data requirements imposed by different countries for the movement of goods. Differing requirements generally require creating separate documents to satisfy export and import controls. Additional documentation is often required to transfer goods at intermediate points.

One might think that the emergence of trading blocs of nations, such as the European Union or NAFTA, would have resulted in harmonized requirements and a reduction in required documentation, but that has not been the case. Systems developed within these economic-based groups continue to be essentially incompatible with one another because of their varied data elements and formatting requirements.

The industry believes that these variations in data requirements increase the risk of errors in data collection and transmission, delaying clearance and creating unwarranted financial liability. Divergent requirements also keep us from exploring ways of processing outbound and inbound clearances with a single filing.

Obviously, under such systems, trade efficiency is curtailed, resulting in:

- greater processing demands on shippers, carriers, and customs;
- reduced performance in clearance of goods; and
- incremental cost increases for all.

Pre-arrival Processes or Expedited Clearance Upon Arrival

Lastly, but possibly most critical in any effort to improve trade efficiency, the industry seeks support for processes that will allow governments to screen consignments en route, and through risk assessment and selectivity, expedite the release of low-risk goods forwarded by known shippers upon arrival.

For this ultimate goal to be realized, the first two points I have raised today will, by necessity, have to be adopted. The benefits of such a program are immediately apparent. By utilizing technological advances, governments would be able to screen consignments in advance of arrival and focus their dwindling inspection resources on those that pose a real threat. The great majority of goods, as much as 99 percent in some countries, could be released for home use with minimum formalities, subject, of course, to periodic, unscheduled checks.

Various methods that can expedite the clearance of goods already exist. Electronic commerce programs can support post-release payment of taxes and duties, which often slows the release of goods cleared in the existing manner. Precedents exist for such schemes. They are based on the shippers' performance and entail adequate financial guarantees and a reliable post-clearance audit procedure.

To further facilitate trade, governments should consider adopting procedures that would allow release documents to be filed electronically from locations other than the airport of importation. Such remote filing procedures would enable shippers and carriers to concentrate their cargo documentation experts in national or regional centers, and would likely result in increased data accuracy, reduced costs, and improved service.

Summary

Many other areas of concern faced by the air transport sector cannot be discussed in this short paper. However, most of them will be resolved by implementing the key solution areas discussed here.

In closing, how does the industry envisage the realization of these solutions? There are no easy answers, but we believe the best opportunities lie with the work being done by the World Customs Organization to revise the Kyoto Convention. That document, when completed and ratified by its contracting parties, will provide customs organizations around the world with a vision for the future and the guidance necessary to solve many of the problems we all face today.

However, to be fully effective as a trade facilitation tool, the Kyoto Convention and all of its annexes must be made obligatory and enforceable on all states. While the WCO is the body that is most competent to revise the Convention, it cannot effectively oversee compliance in the various states.

We firmly believe that the World Trade Organization is best suited for that role, and ask that it undertake this difficult, yet essential, obligation. Without the support of the WTO and other internationally sanctioned governmental bodies, the opportunities for harmonization of requirements and convergence of process, which are so necessary for improved trade facilitation, will continue to be nothing more than a dream.

ANNEXES

Annex I
Survey of Customs Reform and Modernization Trends and Best Practices

World Customs Organization

Introduction

Knowledge as to how the customs environment is evolving and how colleague administrations are managing change can help senior administrators better respond to the challenges ahead. So as to benefit from the collective experience of the membership, the WCO has recently conducted a survey and those results are now available. It is hoped that the results stimulate discussion and reflection on the issue of customs reform and modernization.

The results are an analysis of the responses from 38 countries, or 27 percent of the total WCO membership. This is considered to be a sufficiently valid sample from which to draw indicative conclusions.

We appreciate the contributions from the following members and wish them success in their endeavors to deliver world-class customs services:

Albania	Kazakhstan
Algeria	Latvia
Australia	Lithuania
Austria	Madagascar
Brazil	Malaysia
Canada	Malawi
Chile	Maldives
Cuba	Mexico

Cyprus	Morocco
Czech Republic	New Zealand
Denmark	Norway
Estonia	Philippines
France	Russia
Finland	Senegal
Germany	Turkey
Hungary	United Kingdom
Indonesia	United States
Ireland	Uzbekistan
Italy	Zimbabwe

The experiences and best practices included in this report are those made available by the members for the purpose of this survey.

Trends

Some of the trends described are already emerging; others can be foretold from certain signs. All are supported by experiences and best practices shared by the different members. First, a backdrop against which to view these critical trends for customs executives and officers alike. Three major forces—the proliferation of free-trade agreements, government performance review and rapid technological advances—have profoundly changed, and will continue to change, the nature and content of customs work.

Almost 75 percent of participants indicated that economic integration within the framework of free-trade agreements or customs unions has been a major force in reform. It is noted that the number of regional trading agreements is proliferating. The WTO lists no fewer than 76 free-trade areas or customs unions set up or modified since 1948; more

---

[1] Reprinted in part from the World Customs Organization Web site (www.wcoomd.org) dated October 7, 1997.

than 50 percent have been established in the 1990s.

International liberalization has resulted in booming trade volumes. The WTO estimates that world trade grew by 8 percent in 1995—four times the growth of world GDP. In fact, during the 1990s trade has grown far faster than world output, which indicates that national economies are becoming ever more closely linked. This has been a significant influence in promoting customs modernization particularly in developing/emerging countries where it has been an important driver for 71 percent of the members.

Many governments—66 percent of developing/emerging countries—are considering diversifying existing indirect tax regimes to find other ways of maintaining revenue yield. Increasingly, customs administrations are assigned the responsibility for the administration of all indirect taxes including VAT and excise duties.

Government performance review has pushed up to 60 percent of respondents toward reform and modernization. Budgetary concerns continue to be a major factor in streamlining and "customizing" services.

Increased drugs and security threats are a main issue for 55 percent of developed countries compared with 26 percent for developing/emerging countries.

What Areas Have Been Reformed or Modernized

Change is a continuous process, but in the last five years the pace of change has led to extensive reform and modernization in the customs community.

Eighty-two percent of administrations have been confronted with difficulties caused by archaic legislation. They have reviewed them and sometimes introduced new customs legislation to reflect new priorities and methods of carrying out the customs function.

Information management is also of critical importance for 71 percent of the members surveyed. Technology is now playing an increasing role in the management of information. IT is currently utilized in some countries to assist in customs data management and electronic data interchange.

Sixty-four percent of all administrations surveyed and 89 percent of developed countries have modernized their enforcement strategies and working methods. The changing face of customs enforcement with emphasis on flexible, risk-based and targeted operations accentuates intelligence as the principal weapon to identify fraud and smuggling and the effective deployment of limited resources.

Human resources policies have also been under scrutiny by 61 percent of the members surveyed. Reforms include: recruitment policies, training services role and performance appraisal systems. Many customs administrations have increased the proportion of university graduates in their recruitment programs to support, among other areas, the increasing emphasis on systems-based audits and the use of information technology.

As a result of government performance reviews and changes in the operating environment, more than half of administrations (57 percent) have streamlined their organizations, removed layers of management, gotten closer to their customers. An increasing number of administrations have indicated that they are moving in the direction of a revenue authority (an integrated tax and customs administration).

To aid trade facilitation 57 percent of customs administrations are developing procedures which will expedite clearance of legitimate shipments while accurately targeting irregular transactions.

Thirty-five percent of the members surveyed and almost half of the developing/emerging countries have reviewed their tariffs. According to a recent WCO survey, 77 countries have implemented the 1996 amendments to the HS. These represent 87 percent of the contracting parties.

What Change Management Methods Have Been Successfully Used?

Everyone faces change—the challenge is to manage that change. Those administrations that employ change management principles will have an advantage in implementing wider changes within their organization.

Maintaining two-way communication both inside and outside is a critical success criterion for 76 percent of the members surveyed. Some members even used in-house broadcasts where employees could take part in live television discussions with the Minister and Director General.

Fifty-nine percent of members use outside consultants (65 percent of developing and emerging countries and 44 percent of developed countries). One member pointed out that outside consultants were successfully used only when the customs administration had a clear understanding of what they wanted them to do.

Internal and external focus groups have been the primary methods of defining change requirements for 51 percent of the members surveyed. Many have established permanent structures for consulting stakeholders (groups and individuals who have a specific interest in the business of customs).

Customs role in international trade can be encouraged to combat drug trafficking and other commercial fraud activities. Developing partnerships with trade and other government agencies and closer cooperation between customs administrations themselves have been put in place by 44 percent of members surveyed.

Business process reengineering has been thus far most widely used by developed countries. Sixty-seven percent have reengineered their business processes to enable them to become more efficient and effective, taking into account the impact of their activities on the trading community and the traveling public.

What Are the Future Challenges?

There are still more challenges to come. Here is an outline of what WCO members see as the main influences of customs in the future.

A striking 93 percent of the customs administrations surveyed will try to achieve further gains in efficiency and effectiveness. Some are actually able to operate successfully at costs less than 1 percent of revenue collected.

Attitudinal and organizational cultural change will be necessary. Customs administrations are changing the way they conduct business. More are taking the position that importers and exporters are customers and must be treated as partners, not adversaries. Improving service to customers is for 93 percent of members a major challenge.

In the future, 86 percent of customs administrations will extend their use of technology to include items such as artificial intelligence, bar coding, document imaging. A number of customs administrations are looking at the possibility of further developing electronic communication between customs and business. This will have very significant benefits for customs, as the administration of the future will rely on accurate and timely information in order to carry out its function. Ultimately it is hoped that this could lead to the practical implementation of a "seamless data flow" or, as it is sometimes described, an "integrated data transaction."

According to 82 percent of the members surveyed, the increase in the demand for new skills will lead to the increase in the need for training staff to do new jobs and retraining staff to do jobs differently.

Combating transnational crime is seen as a challenge for 75 percent of the members surveyed, 100 percent for developed countries. The G7 + 1 is alarmed by the growth of organized transnational crime, including money laundering, and have urged countries to adopt necessary legislation.

Success is achieved by those with access to the most

accurate and timely statistical information, according to 68 percent of the respondents. Some are striving to become the main repository of trade data for compiling trade statistics and formulating trade policy.

Integration into free trade and/or customs unions, and thus the development of common tariff and origin rules, will remain a challenge for 75 percent of developing and emerging countries.

What Techniques and Implementation Approaches Are Likely to Play a Pivotal Role in Improving Future Customs Managerial Practices and Performance?

As customs administrations seek to maintain and increase their efficiency and effectiveness, 77 percent favor risk management, which allows for better targeting their resources toward those areas that most warrant attention. By using the principles of risk management, customs administrations will also be able to demonstrate to the government that they are ensuring the best available outcomes for the country within the constraints of the resources they are given.

Seventy percent of the members surveyed intend to use strategic intelligence to support the effective achievement of organizational objectives. In the enforcement context, strategic intelligence will provide executives and senior managers with timely insight into current and emerging trends, threats to public safety and avenues for change in policies, strategies and legislation.

In the past, changes have been brought about by process improvement simplification. Sixty percent of members have indicated that they could go a step further using business process reengineering and examine whether existing processes and structures are really the best way to meet objectives.

Customs administrations are also embarking on a new era of performance measurement (60 percent of members surveyed) as a way of guiding the effectiveness of their initiatives and efforts. More administrations are going beyond cost-based measures to include quality and time-based measures. Some are developing compliance measurements.

Fifty percent of the customs administrations surveyed have or will introduce management audit as a means of quantifying the movement of goods and travelers to aid in allocating resources and to measure results.

Forty-five percent o the respondents are of the opinion that Total Quality Management philosophy and practices will play a pivotal role in customs managerial practices in the years ahead. Some have or will join a National Quality Council; others will go a step further and seek ISO 9000 accreditation for the quality of service that they want to attain in their service function.

Forty percent of the members surveyed say that they are in the process of becoming a learning organization, with the capacity to learn, adapt and change.

The management task will also be different for 28 percent of the members—the focus is increasingly on leading and coaching people toward achieving outcomes, rather than just managing tasks.

What Skills Are Most Likely to Be in Demand

The key to successful future development of customs is to upgrade the professional know-how of its employees. Many of the customs administrations surveyed are creating broad-based skills development programs to enable current and future employees to function better in the customs environment and to equip them to better handle the new techniques and IT systems. More than just traditional training may be needed. Measures such as "apprenticeships," distance learning technologies and the establishment of networks are being considered (chart AI.1).

The increasing reliance on the use of intelligence as a

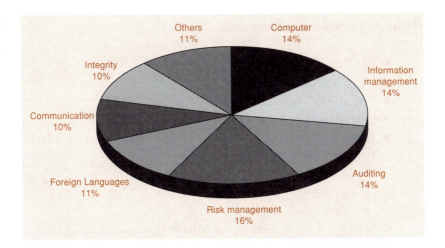

tool for greater selectivity will increase the demand for risk assessment skills.

Computer literacy will be essential for customs officers as information technology becomes an integral part of the workings of the administration and as most of the day-to-day operation becomes dependent on computer-based systems. In addition, personal computers will be used for accounting, word processing and, where the personal computer is connected to a network, for electronic mail.

As customs places greater reliance on postrelease audits, audit skills are going to be required. These skills will need to be incisive and effective to ensure proper compliance.

As more administrations become knowledge-based, information management skills will be increasingly in demand.

Foreign languages will continue to be important with increased internationalization and 55 percent of administrations will enhance their language skills.

Forces That Have Compelled Customs to Reform and Modernize

- People, processes and partnerships (USA)
- Building bridges over turbulent waters (Algeria)

Areas Reformed and Modernized

- EDIFACT (Norway)
- New legislation (Cuba)
- "ACROSS" (Canada)
- Client/server Network (Finland)
- Introduction of a system of guarantees for internal transit of goods (Albania)

Successful Practices

- Hybrid Benchmarking (United Kingdom)
- Personnel Analysis Group (Germany)

Challenges

- Service with a capital "S" (New Zealand)
- Toward world-class service (Philippines)

Techniques and Implementation Approaches

- Risk management (Mexico)
- INGRID (Indicator of Customs' Internal Resources Management) (France)
- Project management (Morocco)

Skills Most Likely in Demand

- Information and training (Czech Republic)

People, Processes and Partnerships (United States)

In October 1993, Commissioner George Weise established a Customs Reorganization Study Team and endowed it with a broad and simple charter: to develop an organizational structure that would enable the US Customs Service and its employees to make their maximum contribution to the nation. In response to that charter a report was produced which recommended management approaches and an organizational structure that would enable Customs to meet the challenges of the 21st century as a more efficient and adaptable organization with high employee involvement.

Being fully aware that demand for service from its customers would continue to increase, and that increases in resources would not keep pace, the study team sought to find ways to move staff from support functions to operational functions. This emphasis on cost avoidance, rather than increases in appropriations, was especially well suited to the national need for deficit reduction balanced with customer service. To that end, the concept of reinvestment was accentuated.

The reinvestment strategy directed available resources toward the resolution of global trade issues, providing increased attention to ensuring voluntary compliance with trade laws through enhanced informed compliance efforts, improving the use of information technology by building on and enhancing Customs' Automated Commercial System, and providing the employee training necessary to enable us to implement process management and customer-focused approaches to the Customs missions.

It was concluded that the number and scope of mission challenges facing the Customs Service, combined with the numerous concerns expressed by employees about the existing management environment, made a compelling case for significantly changing the Customs management structure. In order to achieve the new vision for the Customs Service, to increase its service to the nation and to meet the challenges of the future, it would be necessary to transform Customs' culture to one focusing on people, processes and partnerships. The new culture would characterized by:

- managing essential core processes, a change that would require integrating the many disciplines within the Customs Service into more coordinated efforts to achieve Customs' mission goals;

- serving the legitimate needs of Customs' many customers as the focus of the organization's process management efforts, and forming partnerships with them as a means of meeting their needs and improving Customs' mission performance; and
- building a workforce for the 21st century, working cooperatively to develop strategies to tap the potential of Customs' employees so that, working together, they could meet the mission challenges facing the Customs Service.

To this end, Customs redefined its core processes and has moved to a management approach centered around these processes, identified its customers and their needs, developed methods for defining customers' needs as process goals, improved its workforce through empowerment of its employees and an elevated human resources management program, realigned the organizational structure to reduce layers and support the core processes and reinvested its resources in priority mission areas.

Building Bridges over Turbulent Waters (Algeria)

The new economic policies in Algeria (with, since 1991, a shift away from a controlled and centralized economy toward a market economy) and the globalization of world trade have made Algerian Customs aware that it might well find itself unprepared to face the new external trade rules based on a type of behavior unfamiliar to the vast majority of Customs officials in Algeria.

Thus, change has not been seen as a choice but as an absolute necessity for complete restructuring without which the customs administration was liable to impede economic development and at the same time lose ground with the sudden arrival of new operators and new techniques and rules for supervising international trade.

The administration's strategy for change was laid down in mid-1993. A modernization program was prepared on the basis of a whole series of diagnostic studies carried out by senior Customs staff, who adopted it at a national seminar. This program was presented to the authorities and accepted at an interministerial meeting in November 1993.

The approach decided upon by the Directorate General of Algerian Customs to develop its modernization strategy was centered on:

- identifying the fundamental agents of change;
- introducing strategic management techniques into Customs' management policy; and
- increasing internal communication with staff and social partners so that all shall become stakeholders in the plan to modernize human resources through a wide range of meetings and seminars.

However, the risk of resistance to change, whether internal or from the Customs environment was taken into account in the strategic plan. The Directorate General of Customs has therefore implemented an intensive communication policy aimed at:

- Customs officials, to convince them of the need for the modernization plan, for changes in behavior and culture and for openness to the external environment (universities and higher education/colleges, consultants and experts) on which real improvement in the Customs service and success in overcoming the problems that stem from the sudden liberalization of external trade largely depend;
- public authorities and certain institutions, so that Customs is repositioned as the main state instrument for

implementing the new fiscal, economic and trade policy; and
- public and private economic operators, so that they can be convinced of Customs 'new role as an economic partner and not just a fiscal agent.

EDIFACT (Norway)

The Norwegian Customs Administration implemented its EDIFACT declaration system as early as 1988, and by 1992 the system was available nationwide. Since October 1994, paper-based customs declarations had been manually entered into the electronic clearance system by local Customs authorities. Because of the advantages enjoyed by online users, by 1996, 5 percent of the customs declarations were paper-based and the rest passed through the EDIFACT system.

About 85 percent of the customs declarations pass through the system without being stopped for further investigation. The system is now available to the public on a 24-hour basis, and the average time for the system to clear the goods is 15 minutes. In addition, the quality of the declarations has improved drastically over the last few years.

New Legislation (Cuba)

In Cuba, the present customs organization is the result of a process initiated in 1990 and concluded in April 1996 when the legislation was enacted by the State Council of Cuba.

The legislation was drafted in accordance with universally accepted concepts and practices, including those reflected in the Kyoto Convention of 1973 as well as other World Customs Organization recommendations.

It also strikes a balance between the requirements of control and facilitation in order to ensure that genuine international transit of commodities and travelers is not subjected to unnecessary customs formalities. Risk analysis techniques now make it possible to guarantee facilitation to genuine travelers and consignments without unduly compromising enforcement against illegal activities.

At the same time, the legislation is in agreement with those conventions and agreements referred to under Facilitation for Travelers, Tourists and Temporary Admission of Commodities for exhibits and fairs.

"ACROSS" (Canada) Revenue Canada expands its use of Electronic Data Interchange

Revenue Canada is continuing to do research into new electronic data interchange (EDI) technologies to automate its existing manual, paper-based customs release system.

A new system called the Accelerated Commercial Release Operations Support System (ACROSS), has helped Revenue Canada tailor its programs and services to particular industry sectors and businesses by amalgamating and broadening some of its existing systems to form an integrated EDI system.

ACROSS stems from the Department's New Business Relationship initiative, where programs and services are tailored to particular sectors and business. The system was implemented nationally at all automated customs offices in April 1996.

ACROSS handles customs' reporting and processing needs 24 hours a day, seven days a week. It analyzes release data from clients and recommends whether or not a commercial shipment should be released or examined on the basis of importer compliance profiles and the type of goods. Some of the basic features of the system are :

- EDI release transmission;
- flexible service options for doing business;
- new ways to manage customs' workload between offices across the country;

- automated decision support on the release of goods; and
- capability of identifying high-risk shipments.

EDI systems leading up to ACROSS

ACROSS is not the first EDI system Revenue Canada developed to streamline its customs processes. There are also the following:

- Customs Automated Data Exchange System (CADEX) Customs Declaration Message (CUSDEC), which allows importers and brokers to electronically transmit their accounting data. CADEX\CUSDEC now serves more than 270 clients, making up 86 percent of Canada Customs' commercial business.
- Release Notification System (RNS), which is designed to electronically advise clients that Customs has released their goods.
- Pre-Arrival Release Notification System (PARNS), available 24 hours a day, which allows the carrier to electronically provide Revenue Canada with customs data on shipments in advance of the goods arriving in Canada, permitting pre-arrival review and processing of the data and electronic transmission of a release or refer for examination notification once the goods arrive.
- EDI Cargo System, which allows clients using marine and rail transportation to send their cargo data to customs electronically before the goods arrive. With this system, importers no longer have to present the paper documents with the goods.

ACROSS is being built to move Revenue Canada into the next century. It will be easier and faster for importers who comply with customs laws to have their goods released. At the same time, customs inspectors will be able to target those goods and importers who are high-risk.

Client/Server Network (Finland)

Multilevel organizational structures have been replaced by simpler ones. At the same time activities have become globalized and the organizations form cooperation networks. By using data networks organizations can function irrespective of time and place.

In the customs area in Finland, there will be cooperation networks at least in the following spheres of activity: control of international transport systems, cooperation with police authorities in criminal investigation, sharing of databases of customs administration and agricultural authorities, data interchange between shipping companies, haulers, harbor operators, forwarding agents, importers, exporters and the customs administration.

Within the Finnish Customs administration the solution is a client/server network. The terminals of the Customs personnel are connected to a common network and the Customs officers have access to the systems they may need. It concerns all Customs work including word processing, use of databases, Customs clearance data, payment data, license management as well as common personnel and financial administration systems, management systems and electronic files.

System of Guarantees for Internal Transit Of Goods (Albania)

Prior to 1994 the Customs administration experienced considerable difficulties in accounting for transit consignments. Since then a system of guarantees for internal transit of goods has been introduced. Under this system internal transit consignments must be covered by any one of the following guarantees:

- personal guarantee (cash guarantee);
- Customs broker guarantee consisting of a letter of guarantee lodged with Customs by a licensed broker (to be licensed for this purpose a broker should lodge a blanket bank guarantee in favor of Customs to cover all its operations);
- banking guarantee, which means that a bank, or any third party authorized by the bank, gives a written guarantee in respect of an importer of exporter;
- insurance guarantee, which means that an insurance company guarantees that an operator will make Customs clearance at the place of destination.

This approach suits the country very well. At present, there are few Customs offenses in dealing with internal transit.

Hybrid Benchmarking (United Kingdom)

Benchmarking is a systematic method to improve performance by measuring and comparing products, services and processes against the best. It is used widely in the private sector for competitor analysis; as a quality tool; to drive down costs; and as an efficiency tool. However, HM Customs and Excise interest lies in its use as an efficiency tool to deliver value for money services.

It was decided that the way forward was to develop a technique that utilized a high level approach to benchmarking within a structure similar to that of a market test. We named the new technique "hybrid benchmarking" and defined it as:

An efficiency technique which compares departmental performance in chosen areas with public and private sector performance in similar areas using a structure similar to that of a market test.

The hybrid benchmarking technique provides a structured approach focused on the delivery of efficiency savings and improvements to quality; a method of ensuring that efficiency improvements are put in place and delivered through Service Level Agreements; a method of comparing price and quality through the identification of best practice; access for private sector involvement through the use of consultants; involvement for all the staff concerned in the process without the fear inherent in market testing that jobs may transfer to the private sector and a process that can be used in core and noncore areas.

Results of hybrid benchmarking

In 1995 1996, exercises were conducted in all the departments regional units and headquarters. The activities examined included typing, personnel management, information technology support, accounts and finance, premises management and VAT Control Unit (processing returns).

In all, nearly fifty exercises were conducted covering 1,300 posts, with a total annual value of £ 30 million. The results of these exercises were remarkably similar to those using market testing with average savings of around 20 percent, with the standard of service being at least maintained and, in many cases, improved.

Personnel Analysis Group (Germany)

One of the main objectives of the customs administration is to make the administration more economical and efficient. The corresponding initiatives for the realization of the model of a "lean state" provide for creating larger administrative units and broader fields of work in order to facilitate concentration of tasks and a greater degree of specialization of the work force. Larger units, capable of specialization, are thus clearly accorded priority over small, "all-round" units.

At the same time, efforts to achieve greater economy in administrative action focus on the centralization of tasks, the optimization of work-flows and progressive utilization of informational technology (IT) as well as efficiency reviews of government activity including the possibility of transferring some tasks and functions outside the administration.

In order to optimize operational procedures and determine manpower requirements in line with the tasks to be done, in 1990 the customs administration created what are known as Personnel Analysis Groups. These groups have the job of conducting functional analyses for individual fields of work on the basis of recognized ergonomic methods, examining organizational structures and work-flows and producing work statistics, in order to lay down operational procedures and plan personnel requirements. The work of these groups therefore makes a significant contribution to ensuring and increasing the effectiveness and efficiency of administrative action.

Service with a Capital "S" (New Zealand)

It's a word that many organizations bandy about and, for a lot of people, seems to be no more than the latest nineties buzzword—especially if you've had bad service from a so called service organization.

But for New Zealand Customs, "service" has been taken so much to heart that it's soon to be known as the New Zealand Customs Service.

"That one word underscores our values," says Comptroller Graeme Ludlow. "Service to the Government as a collector and enforcer, and service to New Zealand business and individuals in terms of meeting their expectations. Our aim is to get a good fit between the two types of service, and to do the best we can for both Government and New Zealand.

"By having a client focus we will be able to develop initiatives that meet their needs within the limits imposed by the law. It will bring Customs into the late 20th Century, and is part of a whole revamp of everything we do. The new Act will help us use our customer focus, as will our modernization project, but we see client focus as involving everything from the Act to little things like redesigning public counter areas.

"For example, New Zealand is no longer an eight to five, Monday to Friday country. We need to reflect that. We also need to be more approachable—for us, service means giving people answers to questions rather than just telling them what the procedures are."

Mr. Ludlow says that putting the word "Service" in the name gets the message through to everyone—inside and outside the organization. That message is: Customs is only there to provide a service to New Zealand society.

Towards World-Class Service (Philippines)

As the Philippines Bureau of Customs[1] moves toward the 21st century, it sees for itself a Vision for its preferred future. Inspired by the common desire to make the Philippine Customs Service truly a world class Customs Service. Our concepts of a successfully implemented modernization initiative are the following:

- *Image.* Held in high esteem in the public view, its role for national development and international trade facilitation shall be imbued in the hearts and minds of every Customs official and staff as the Bureau moves forward in its other roles of promoting national security, justice, health and other objectives.
- *Stakeholders.* A truly professional relationship should exist between customs and industry. It shall attain a high level of cooperation and it sees itself even closer

---

[1] The Philippines' customs modernization program is described in detail in chapter 7.

to its clientele through the provision of appropriate machinery for communicating suggestions, complaints and other form of feedback.

- *Targets, policies and procedures.* It shall be capable of processing all documents electronically within minutes and be able to release goods in a matter of hours as its computerization moves forward to advanced state of electronic commerce. It sees itself adopting international standards for procedures, forms and coding and sees exceptionally good working relationship with the legislature so that laws are more responsive to the demands of modernization.

- *Organization and people.* It shall advance toward a streamlined organization characterized by decentralized management and control as well as a leaner but better paid staff.

- *Resources.* In order to provide quality service to the business community while generating maximum revenue for government, the Bureau shall be equipped with modern building facilities and office equipment. It shall have sufficient land, air and water transport resources to assist in its operation and it shall use state of the art technology to cope with the changing trade environment for the next millennium.

Risk Management (Mexico)

Mexican Customs uses an intelligent aleatory system which determines whether or not goods will be inspected. The system relies on data such as country of origin, importer, exporter, type of merchandise, tariff item number, etc., loaded into its database to determine whether a particular passenger of consignment must be inspected.

Upon completion of customs formalities in respect of a passenger or a consignment the system is interrogated by the pressing the appropriate button. In 90 percent of the time the green light flashes indicating that no further formalities are required. Consequently, only 10 percent of passengers or consignments are chosen for inspection.

Unlike with other systems, this system is not entirely at random as it uses information in its database to determine the level of risk. This kind of risk management system has proved to be very successful to Mexican Customs and has a good impact in public image as well as in revenue.

INGRID (Indicator of Customs Internal Resources Management) (France)

The French Customs Administration is going to set up a database accessible to the offices of both the Directorate General and the regional directorates. The server, called INGRID (Indicateur de Gestion des Ressources Internes de la Douane, Indicator of Customs' Internal Resources Management), contains data from two user programs. One program records, on a half-yearly basis, a number of indicators relating to Customs resources, the Customs environment and the results and activities of the various departments, while the other covers the use of the departments' operating funds, whose management is the responsibility of the regional director.

In bringing all this data together, INGRID constitutes a real management control system for evaluating the service's efficiency, the suitability of the organizational methods chosen and the cost of various missions.

The departments can consult some fifty tables on the most frequent studies. Using specialized software they can also conduct any specific studies as required.

Project Management (Morocco)

Since April 1995, the Ministry of Finance and Foreign Investment has been involved in a huge modernization program affecting several areas of activity.

This program revolves around the following four main strategic axes:

- achieving greater openness to the Ministry's clients and partners by taking account of their expectations and by promoting the concept of "public service";
- seeking efficiency in the areas of the Ministry's activity by optimization of human, material and financial resources in Ministry headquarters and external services;
- motivating all the Ministry officials to support the modernization plan by adapting the management plan and by progressively improving working conditions; and
- ensuring that the Ministry's working practices keep pace with developments in the national and international environment.

An action plan had been developed to attain these objectives, comprising not only short-term actions aimed principally at establishing a climate for change, but also reform projects which should in the long term result in the restructuring of the Ministry and improvements in its operation.

The structuring reform projects are as follows:

- clarifying the Ministry's missions and adapting the way it is organized;
- designing a system for evaluating client service;
- reforming the rules through process logic;
- upgrading procedures;
- drawing up a global strategic steering plan for the Ministry's information systems and for the organization of the ADP system;
- implementing forward-looking management of human resources and establishing a training plan;
- developing an internal performance evaluation system;

- improving and optimizing working conditions;
- preparing a communication plan; and
- adapting the styles of management.

The need for these reforms led the Administration of Customs and Indirect Taxation, as a Directorate of the Ministry, to adopt them and include them in its action plan.

A study was conducted to that end. It diagnosed the following seven strategic areas on the basis of which a general program was prepared:

- legislation and procedures;
- customs economic procedures;
- taxation;
- enforcement;
- organization and human resources;
- automatic data processing (ADP); and
- logistics.

To carry out this program successfully and to ensure that it is implemented in accordance with the commitments undertaken by each section of the Directorate General, a Programs and Evaluation Section was set up whose main task is to monitor and manage a system for programming and evaluating the administration.

This system has two pillars : a planning pillar and an evaluation pillar.

Planning pillar

For the seven areas of reform mentioned above, plans setting out the actions and tasks of each section were prepared and approved by the Management Committee comprising Directors and Deputy Directors from Headquarters.

For each activity or task chosen, the plan gives the start and finishing date and name the officer in charge.

Evaluation pillar

Once the action plan was defined, a very simple monitoring mechanism was put in place. It consists of sending the section heads a monthly table in which they mark a score for their action's progress.

Once the tables are completed by the relevant section heads, they are returned to the Planning and Evaluation Service which studies the results.

Evaluation is the responsibility of the services initiating the action.

The planning and evaluation pillars are managed using software installed in a PC.

Information and Training (Czech Republic)

In preparation for the Czech Republic's Membership of the European Union, the main priority is the establishment of efficient Customs Information System. Having been under development for the past six years, the CIS now incorporates the automatic processing of all basic Customs procedures in all Customs offices, daily data transfer for central processing via a satellite and a quick distribution of the integrated tariffs through its communication system.

Another important issue in the modernization process was the modification of the training system to reflect the changing needs of the Czech Customs Administration. The change was successfully implemented and produced very positive results.

Annex II
Compendium of Trade Facilitation Recommendations

United Nations Conference on Trade and Development (UNCTAD) UN/ECE Working Party on Facilitation of International Trade Procedures (WP.4)

Foreword

This Compendium has been compiled within the UNCTAD Special Programme for Trade Efficiency (SPTE) as a contribution to the work being done by the ECE Working Party on Facilitation of International Trade Procedures (WP.4) in preparation for the 1994 United Nations International Symposium on Trade Efficiency. It is intended to be used as reference material by those engaged, at the national, sectorial or international level, in the process of simplifying and rationalizing trade procedures in a broad sense, and also by trade operators which would be looking for model practices, agreed standards, etc., that could serve as a basis for improving their procedures and modus operandi.

The Introduction contains background information on the fundamental and practical issues that Trade Facilitation addresses; it is based on a study made by SITPRO, the Simpler Trade Procedures Board of the United Kingdom. The Introduction reviews the present situation in the field of the production, transfer and use of information required in the course of an international trade transaction, with a view

Taken from UNCTAD, WP.4, July 1993, Geneva.

to identifying the needs for further harmonization, standardization and simplification for more efficient trade. Examples are given of some of the practical solutions which are the subject of Recommendations by WP.4 or other bodies, and of problems which still have to be solved.

For many years, in addition to specific Trade Facilitation Recommendations like those adopted by WP.4, international instruments being developed in areas connected with international trade and transport have incorporated provisions aimed at facilitating the movement of goods and means of transport or the provision of services by reducing information requirements, streamlining procedures, standardizing information elements and paper forms, harmonizing official and commercial practices, providing standard formats for electronic transmission. The objectives and scope of these various instruments are briefly presented in the sources page.

The Recommendations are listed by both group and index. They contain the complete or abridged text, or a paraphrase, as appropriate, of the Recommendations. These extracts from international instruments are given for reference purposes, and not as a substitute for the full text which constitutes the only valid source for official use.

Information Flows

Formalities, procedures and paperwork in international trade are generated by the need for both governments and trade operators to monitor and control the movement of goods and the transfer of services and by the necessity of safeguarding every party's legitimate interests. Closely related to this are the requirements for information and financial flows between the trading parties. Over the years, trade facilitation efforts conducted by international or national bodies in various countries or sectors have introduced improvements in the trade-related information flows, by simplifying the requirements, harmonizing the procedures and the documentation, standardizing commercial practices, introducing agreed codes for the representation of information elements. However, certain countries still maintain requirements which run contrary to these facilitation efforts, because of historical precedents, commercial inertia, difficulty in adjusting the methods of their control bodies, or ignorance of the solutions that have been developed elsewhere.

The systems developed to link the shippers, transport operators, port authorities, bankers, insurance companies, Customs, consignees and others concerned in the business of international trade are constantly being adapted to meet the changing needs associated in particular with the speed of modern transport and express freight deliveries and the convenience attainable through the use of containers, and also to take advantage of the possibilities that technology offers for improving information processing and transmission.

Today information flows are at a point midway between paper documents still often painfully filled in by hand, those produced by computer but still sent manually (and often re-entered manually into another computer) and the world of automatic data transmission where data are sent from computer to computer with minimal human intervention.

The timely arrival of information is a vital component in any international trade transaction; but frequently the goods arrive at the destination before the information needed by the operators to perform their function. Delays in information production and transfer can be reduced if agreement is reached to make the maximum use of modern information technology, e.g. computerizing the preparation of required documents, sending copies by facsimile transmission, or using Electronic Data Interchange (EDI). Where this is too far advanced, the use of standard aligned documents can provide a solution for simplifying document preparation. However more needs to be done to facilitate the information flows (i.e. how the data are collected, transferred and dealt with). While part of the answer may lie in the simplification of the official and commercial procedures themselves, there should be in addition some systematic way of handling information relevant to the technology available. The advent of cheap and reliable computers even in the least advanced countries offers enormous opportunities. So does the progress achieved in telecommunications facilities.

The problems created by trade documents and procedures fall into two categories: the supply of data; and the complexity of some of the procedures. As stated above goods often arrive before the information which should precede them and which is essential if they are to be dealt with expeditiously. Some companies take very expensive solutions, e.g. the use of courier services, to avoid delays due to missing documents at critical points in the transaction chain. However, this can be efficient only if despatches are adjusted to the speed of the best practical performance that can be expected in average international transactions. The complexity of some of the procedures may greatly increase the loss of efficiency if steps are not taken to minimize the amount of information required while goods are in transit. More generally, procedural requirements should be re-examined and manual systems tidied up before information technology can, with safety and economic advantage, be systematically applied.

In theory, there should be nothing inherently too complicated in the systems and procedures for selling goods from one country to another. Indeed, apart from additional official requirements caused by the protection of national interests, this should replicate the procedures carried out in any domestic market. The difficulties arise in part from the sheer scale of the operations and in part from the vast number of people, interests, nations and languages involved. What may appear as a facilitation solution in one part of this network can, and often does, create difficulties in another. To take an example, Preshipment Inspection (PSI), which may be appropriate to solve a specific problem in the importing country, can impede the exporter, and the latter incorporates the costs incurred into his selling price; the resulting costs of PSI are finally borne by the final consumer of the goods in the importing country.

Buyer and seller want to see their agreement for the sale and purchase of goods accomplished with the minimum of complication and cost against the background of their total production control and marketing arrangements. The seller wants sure payment and a safe timely arrival of his goods so that a single transaction is not only satisfactory to both parties but also contributes to the possibility of future business. The buyer wants to receive the goods he has agreed to buy at the place and time provided in his contract in good condition and with no more formalities or exertion on his part than are reasonably necessary to obtain possession and make payment.

Carrying and handling interests want to be able to receive and deliver the goods on behalf of their clients with the minimum of complication. They also seek to fulfil this function in ways and under conditions conforming as closely as possible with their own requirements for the effective operation of their transport and handling resources.

The banker wants to finance and facilitate payment for his customers' trade transactions by means which, while meeting individual requirements as closely as possible, will give proper weight to prudent precautions against loss or misunderstanding. In this he needs the prompt presentation of documents which comply with the terms of the instructions he has received. Any variation in the documents, particularly when payment is made in the framework of a Documentary Credit, will result in delays for correction or verification.

However reasonable and economically justified such needs are, it is by no means uncommon for the requirements of one commercial concern or trade to conflict with those of another. Individual needs and incompatibilities must be identified before they can be reconciled and reconciled before they can be met. The best people to explain their needs will always be the commercial interests themselves, but this requires that they have ample means of expressing their views through a variety of organizations, including national trade facilitation bodies, as recommended by the UN/ECE Working Party on Facilitation of International Trade Procedures (WP.4).

As mentioned above, the requirements of both governments and commercial operators to monitor and control the movement of goods and payment thereof drive the procedures and paperwork generated in international trade. Whilst the ultimate destination of the information may be divided between the official and commercial sectors, during the transaction the data required by both sectors remain closely and inextricably linked. Commercial requirements are devised by the trading parties to meet their own needs and are therefore malleable and easily adaptable to comply with changing trade practices. By contrast, official requirements are enforced and controlled by governments and have diverse aims, such as fiscal, protective, trade control and health requirements. The facilitation of trade may not be the primary purpose so the possibility of change can be limited or at the best very slow.

Those asking for and those providing information each have certain responsibilities. The essence of the technical task is to move minimum information with maximum efficiency. The criterion should be the minimum information necessary to service the transaction and not the minimum that people would like to obtain for other purposes. This puts a special responsibility on those interests, especially governments, banks and other credit institutions, which are in a position to enforce their data requirements.

Regardless of the end use of the data, the timely arrival of information, certainly before the arrival of the goods, is a vital component in any international trade transaction. As world distances "shrink" and travel times are reduced, it is essential that information is transmitted using the quickest, most effective method available to the parties involved. If it arrives after the cargo, the best information in the world will still cause acute problems, especially in the port community. Whilst it is appreciated that the technology available in different parts of the world may differ, where possible the use of modern technology should be encouraged, and suitable conditions for such use (including the necessary legal or regulatory framework) should be established in the countries concerned.

Documentary Requirements

One of the arguments commonly stated against the paperwork and procedures in international trade is that they may give rise to avoidable costs, e.g., those concerning duplication and reproduction of data, a problem which is greatly accentuated when a transaction is not perfectly executed.

Costs in this crude sense may be an ambiguous and even misleading index. Effective overall control systems might be established which, while showing substantial advantages at the management center, could impose extra complications and costs on shipping and movement control functions taken in isolation.

Given that massive information is required in international trade, which can result in a mass of paper, there are attractions in any method which can simplify the production of the numbers and copies of documents. Many of the difficulties associated with information flows can be eliminated by the use of "aligned documents," i.e., documents printed on the same size paper and with common items of information set out in the same relative position on each form.

Although the range of documents aligned to a common standard, the United Nations Layout Key, is now fairly extensive, many companies do not avail themselves of this facility. They should be made aware of the benefits they could derive from using aligned documents, the more so if internal company requirements are also linked to the aligned system.

The basic system is very simple and can operate without modern technology. By typing the details of the transaction or shipment on a master document, the aligned forms can be prepared by what is known as the "one-run" system. Various methods of reproduction can be used-spirit duplicating, dyeline and, more commonly, photocopying. Items of information which are not required on individual forms for a particular procedure can be omitted by the use of plastic masks or other techniques, which blank out the data on the reproduced document.

Information can be added to the master document at any time during the preparation and printing of individual forms. These systems reduce the cost and time taken to prepare documents and, once the master has been checked, ensure that the information on all forms is accurate.

Software packages are also available for extracting the required information from internal databases and producing aligned documents using microcomputers. This enables the companies either to produce masters which are used for reproducing the required forms, to print information on preprinted forms, or to produce completed forms from plain paper by using a laser printer.

In considering reforms in documentation and procedures, commercial interests will be much influenced by likely effective reductions in the overall cost of financing, handling and moving goods from exporter to importer, seller to buyer. It should be realized in this respect that the direct costs of documents and procedures are only one part of the story. Indirect costs, such as fines, demurrage and loss of business because of inadequate documentation, which can be far more significant, are difficult if not impossible to cost in advance or quantify. Documentation and procedural costs in a particular transaction may be minimal yet any one of the many minor errors which are endemic throughout present systems, may result for example, in demurrage costs of thousands of dollars.

In this context, those asking for information, e.g., Customs, carriers, etc., should ask for the minimum of information at the best time and, if asking others to complete their documents (e.g. goods declarations), provide these in a standard format. Those providing information have a responsibility to provide accurate data at the right time on the agreed format. When these conditions are fulfilled, each party—both the provider and receiver of information—can operate efficient documentation systems and carry out their own procedures in the minimum time.

Electronic Data Interchange (EDI)

EDI is a product of the two most rapidly advancing technologies in modern times, namely computing and telecommunications. The convergence of these two technologies has made it possible for a structured string of data to be exchanged between business applications without human intervention. EDI revolutionizes business communications by removing a complete layer in business practices—the use and processing of paper documents. The rationalization of data flows within a company enhances the integration of business functions and hence facilitates the decision making process. EDI opens up potent strategies such as "just in time" manufacturing. In addition, it enables companies to forge closer and more effective links with their trading partners.

Paperless trading is growing fast in many countries, in particular because "just in time" stock control usually means more, smaller shipments with very tight delivery schedules that paper documents cannot cope with, and also because EDI is a natural evolution in the international trade cycle. Indeed, one of the principal reasons for using EDI is the mountain of paper documents produced, moved, handled, corrected, transcribed and copied in normal business transactions. EDI has none of the disadvantages of paper documents and brings substantial benefits and savings to companies which implement it, such as accuracy (data are received directly from computer files and are not re-entered manually), speed (data are processed by computer without manual intervention and are transmitted quicker than information sent by post or courier and reentered manually) and savings (it saves on the cost of mailing, copying, filing, distributing and capturing data).

EDI cannot function without standards. Among the standards necessary for doing EDI, those concerning message construction are similar to a language, consisting of a syntax, i.e. rules for structuring data elements in segments within a message, and a vocabulary of words (data elements directory). Differing EDI standards have developed to meet sectorial and national requirements for a speedy and successful implementation within closed groups, but implementation across national and sectorial boundaries (open EDI) is difficult, since partners have to be able to support, maintain and interpret several EDI standards at great expense and inconvenience.

To remedy this, for more than ten years the UN/ECE WP.4 has been developing essential standards covering data elements, codes and syntax rules for EDI. UN/EDIFACT, the result of this development, provides the world market with the necessary ingredients for constructing EDI messages, as well as with complete standard message types (UNSMs) for business data interchange.

It is obvious that replacing paper documents by EDI messages does not change the basic trade requirements between partners in international trade transactions. The same fundamental functions should be fulfilled, and the partners will still be, through EDI, sending and receiving a purchase order, or declaring goods to Customs, or reserving space with a carrier and arranging payments. For international trade information flows, it is the way in which data are transferred that will permit substantial procedural rationalization, and a more efficient trade, as is already the case, for example, in the framework of community systems largely based on the use of information technology, including EDI. In some countries, this may necessitate changes in laws and regulations, e.g., for permitting the replacement of traditional paper documents, Customs declarations, etc., by electronic messages, or for giving such messages the same legal value as that of a paper document.

Cargo/Goods Requirements

Each sector in the international trade cycle needs to identify consignments uniquely; for example Customs need to know precisely which goods have been declared for examination and control purposes; port authorities, container depot operators and wharfingers need to know exactly which goods they have authority to deliver from their charge; shipping lines need to itemize and account for goods which they carry; importers and exporters need to know precisely which of their goods are in transit and for which to arrange for carriage and handling payments.

Currently it is rare in ports and container depots for a single consignment reference to appear on both the cargo and the associated documentation as a unique identifier. It is important that those who handle or examine goods are able to recognize and separate one consignment from another. The marks and numbers together with the description and the number of packages fulfil the requirement.

As a result, regardless of the mode of transport, goods moved internationally by conventional methods still require physical markings which are also reproduced in related documents and transmitted as data elements in EDI. The purpose of a shipping mark is to identify cargo and help in moving it rapidly, smoothly and safely, without delays or confusion, to its final destination and to enable the checking of cargo against documents. However, in many instances marks have become so lengthy and detailed that the sides of packages themselves can no longer hold them or can they be understood. The result is unnecessary costs, mistakes, confusion and shipment delays.

Shipping marks differ widely between countries and between modes of transport. With the increasing volume of international trade, the advent of multimodal and combined transport, the growing need to manage such data (whether in paper based systems or using EDI) and with increasing costs consciousness, it is clear that simple and consistent standards should be applied for physical marking of goods. Such is the purpose of ECE/FAL Recommendation No. 15 "Simpler Shipping Marks."

Linked closely to the need for a Simpler Shipping Mark is the requirement for a single referencing system. In international trade the different parties involved in a transaction each create and receive numerous references on documents, in shipping marks and EDI messages. The current referencing systems, while being purposeful to the generator, mean little or nothing to a third party who in turn generates its own reference. In an international trade transaction, up to thirty or more references can be generated, all of which are usually held in some form of data base. With the development of EDI, it becomes obvious that these many references are expensive to store and transfer and a method has to be found to replace them.

To that effect, the UN/ECE WP.4 has developed in 1992 a (revised) ECE/FAL Recommendation No. 8, the Unique Identification Code Methodology (UNIC), which proposes a method for referencing a transaction or consignment for the totality of its existence. It can be generated by either the buyer, the seller or provider of service and can be used by both official and commercial organizations. It complies with UN/EDIFACT and UN documentary standards and has the specific function of becoming the only reference in international and, potentially, national trade. The current Recommendation relies on existing codes and references issued by commercial coding agencies, official bodies such as fiscal or statistical authorities, and trading companies themselves. The system is totally generic and can be bar-coded with the appropriate symbologies.

Official Requirements

Many of the documents and procedures required in international trade have been devised by commercial interests to meet their own commercial requirements. Even when they are out of date or inappropriate for changed circumstances (e.g., changes in transport methods), they are at least designed to facilitate trade, whereas government requirements, and the documentation and procedures which stem from them, have diverse aims and the facilitation of trade may not be their primary purpose. However, in many countries, the trade may be aware of an almost continuous process review, in particular by Customs, to meet the demands of new methods of trade and transport and to increase the efficiency and effectiveness of control services. This results in part from a progressive implementation of the provisions of the Kyoto Convention of the Customs Cooperation Council , and also from the introduction of automated systems like the UNCTAD ASYCUDA, or of Customs EDI facilities, in an always increasing number of countries.

Customs agencies tend to be responsible for the application of a wide variety of measures the basic policies of which are determined by other government departments. For instance, they enforce exchange control regulations and import and export restrictions and prohibitions; they ensure compliance with certain public health regulations; they compile trade statistics and collect certain levies on behalf of other agencies.

Willingness by Customs to modify their requirements in no way relieves exporters of their obligation to make accurate declarations for exported goods, and importers of their obligation to ensure the speedy release of the goods by meeting the necessary detailed Customs requirements for information and documents. In many countries now, Customs are willing to accept telex or telefaxed information, either in lieu of packing lists or as temporary substitute for an invoice, and will release imported goods accordingly. Nevertheless, errors by importers continually hinder the swift clearance of goods. Analysis of representative samples of import entries show that some 20–30 percent of them are incorrect in at least one respect. Typical errors are omission of essential information, incorrect tariff or statistical classification, and failure to produce supporting documents. Again, the use of the aligned system of documents and of EDI should ensure such occasions are reduced.

These errors can have a considerable effect on the service Customs are able to provide. For instance, trader performance is often taken into consideration by Customs for granting greater facilities and accelerated procedures. Such facilities include Customs clearance undertaken at the traders' premises, based on qualifying criteria of movement and trader performance, or simpler Customs documentation linked to audit based controls.

Harmonization of Customs data in the area of product classification has been achieved by the introduction of the CCC International Convention on the Harmonized Commodity Description and Coding System (HS). The HS was created to meet a vital and pressing need for a single classification system which would respond to the basic commodity description and coding requirements of the entire international trade community. Countries using the HS account for over 85 percent of world trade. However, one of the basic objectives of the HS, with its multi-purpose features, is to apply the classification code outside the Customs environment, i.e. to ensure its application not only by Customs and statisticians but also by commercial interests such as traders, carriers and producers. This objective is far from being attained, and every effort should be made to ensure that this genuine business opportunity is not lost.

Payment Procedures

Payment is an essential parameter in international trade. The method of payment and its efficiency is influenced not only by commercial practices but also, in some countries, by government policy.

Methods of payment are sometimes not as efficient as they should be because of exchange control regulations imposed by the government in the country of import, or because traders are not fully conversant with the implications of certain methods, or because they wish to over protect the payment. These restrictions are generally counter productive and result in deterring rather than encouraging trade.

One of the most widely used methods is the Letter of Credit (L/C). The Documentary Credit system which has been in use for over a hundred and fifty years was introduced to provide payment against proper presentation of documents. L/Cs are used for consignments of both very low and very high value, even though for low value consignments this method is not always economically justifiable.

The requirements for a L/C vary considerably throughout the world, the more difficult cases being associated with developing countries. For example, a credit from one of those countries could well be expected to consist of four pages of requirements, which must be strictly adhered to, and are often contradictory.

Research in the United Kingdom has also indicated that in over 50 percent of cases, the documents which had to be presented to secure settlement were rejected on first presentation because of defects or errors which made them unacceptable according to the terms of credit. Not surprising, this was found largely to be due to reliance on manual processing and the rewriting or rekeying of information.

Credit requirements are also affected by interpretation of language. This is especially evident where, under the terms of the credit, transhipment is prohibited. Although defined in the Uniform Customs and Practice for Documentary Credits (UCP) of the International Chamber of Commerce (ICC), the term transhipment is sometimes interpreted in different ways, and this can result in the credit being void. Similar difficulties may be caused by misunderstandings between buyer and seller. Frequently the buyer will specify a condition, e.g., "shipped on deck," which may have a particular interpretation to him whilst to the seller it has a conflicting meaning. If parties do not agree on the conditions beforehand, the discrepancy may come to light at the time of presentation to the bank when the possibility for amendment is limited. Although the ICC has produced the above mentioned UCP (recently revised and issued as "UCP 500"), (the UCP 500 are referred to on various occasions in group O) some countries insist on referring to their standard banking practice, which is specific to that country and often not definitive.

As well as methods of payment, the methods of remittance of funds are also important. These methods range from the S.W.I.F.T. Express Money Transfers (EMTs) to postal cheques, and delays in the system vary considerably. It is not untypical for a payment transfer to take up to thirty days and, in interest costs alone, it can amount to a considerable sum. From a buyer's standpoint remittance times are not beneficial as the sum has already been removed from his account. All major banks openly state that it is not their policy to retard money transfers nor retain traders' money any longer than absolutely necessary. Nevertheless, in almost all international trade transactions where money passes from buyer to seller, more than one bank is involved in the money transfer and delays occur, which are often caused by technological flaws or human error.

Delays can be reduced by using efficient and fast remittance systems such as EMTs, but the cost for using these systems could be prohibitive: At present it would not be economical to use EMTs for sums of less than USD 10,000 as the cost would exceed the benefits. This directly affects international trade efficiency and has particular implications for the smaller international trader who relies heavily on cash flow.

An additional and very frequent cause for delays stems from strict Exchange Control regulations in a number of countries, which impose certain payment methods (like the compulsory use of L/Cs whilst other more flexible methods such as bills of exchange or open accounts could be used in many instances, e.g., when the transaction takes place between established and trusted partners). Mandatory requirements in letter of credit payments, e.g., the requirement for PSI, may result in additional delays when the Inspection Certificate is not issued or transmitted in time by the Inspection company. In practice, such official requirements may be particularly onerous to the trader and do impede trade information flows. They can actively discourage trade with certain countries where the requirements are too stringent. It would obviously be beneficial for these countries to study how their legitimate objective, i.e. to protect their scarce resources in hard currencies and, in some instances, to control the repatriation of export proceeds, could be attained through methods that would not delay normal payments between trade partners.

Conclusion

In the same manner as the speed of a convoy is determined by that of the slowest truck or ship, or the strength of a chain by that of its weakest link, trade efficiency cannot be reached if one operator in the transaction chain does not operate efficiently. This goes for both private parties and government agencies controlling the movement of goods in international trade.

It is therefore essential that trade procedures and practices are governed by universally agreed basic principles and norms that could be applied by all participants in the transaction, irrespective of their methods of intervention and the degree of sophistication of their information management systems. There is no doubt that the use of electronic techniques for information transfer, and in particular EDI, will significantly contribute to a more efficient trade; however, it should be realized that this objective will be attained only if the basic procedures are in order in the exporting as well as the importing country.

Tools for devising efficient procedures are available in the form of standards, recommended practices, model procedures, etc. The Compendium of Trade Facilitation Recommendations includes a comprehensive list of such practical measures. Although there are no recent indications concerning the extent to which they are actually implemented in the individual countries, it is well known that most of these tools are extensively used in a large number of countries at various levels of development; they have proven their efficiency. Many of them are fundamental for the streamlining of international trade procedures; their generalized application would be a formidable step forward towards more efficient trade through better practices.

Annex III
Summary of Efforts by ASEM & Japan Towards Trade facilitation

PRESENTATION BY
Hiroshi Arichi

ASEM

- European Commission
- 15 member states
- ASEAN
- China
- Korea
- Japan

Source: Customs and Tariff Bureau, MOF, Japan

TFAP
Trade Facilitation Action Plan

- Framework agreed at ASEM EMM at Makuhari, Japan in September 1997
- TFAP adopted at ASEM II in London, April 1998

Source: Customs and Tariff Bureau, MOF, Japan

TFAP (Customs area) (1)

- Accelerated alignment and harmonization of tariff nomenclatures with the WCO standards
- accelerated implementation of obligations under the WTO Customs Valuation Agreement
- endeavour to start negotiations on customs cooperation and mutual administrative assistance agreements between the European Community and the interested ASEM Asian partner

Source: Customs and Tariff Bureau, MOF, Japan

TFAP (Customs area) (2)

- promotion of transparency through mutual access to each ASEM partners' existing databases such as customs duties and nomenclature, tariff quotas, import and export procedures and formalities, rules of origin, customs legislation, etc.
- Improvement of predictability for the business community through publication and clarification upon request, of customs regulations and procedures in force taking into account, where appropriate, the relevant international customs conventions, such as the Kyoto Convention

Source: Customs and Tariff Bureau, MOF, Japan

TFAP (Customs area) (3)

- organization of ASEM seminars for customs and business representatives, in close consultation with the Asia-Europe Business Forum (AEBF), and including, for example, key issues such as risk analysis, EDI, paperless systems and speeding-up of the customs handling
- promotion of standardized and simplified documentation taking into account the existing international standards and the on-going duscussions in various international fora

Source: Customs and Tariff Bureau, MOF, Japan

TFAP (Customs area) (4)

- where appropriate, the exploration of possible common positions of ASEM partners in WTO and WCO
- taking into account resources available, provide possible technical assistance and training programmes related to customs simplified procedures that will contribute to ASEM expertise and experience

Source: Customs and Tariff Bureau, MOF, Japan

The survey on the time required for the release of goods

Purposes
- To identify cause(s) of delay in the entire clearance process.
- To examine the effects of mesures taken for improvement/ facilitation.

Source: Customs and Tariff Bureau, MOF, Japan

Flow Chart of Import Procedures

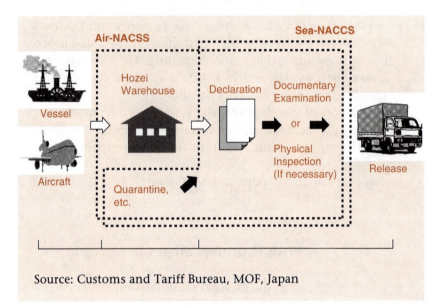

Source: Customs and Tariff Bureau, MOF, Japan

Time required for the Customs clearance

Survey		Reduction in time	
		(Air)	(Sea)
• 1st: February	1991	2.3h	26.1h
• 2nd: February	1992		
• 3rd: March	1993	(–70%)	(–79%)
• 4th: March	1996	↓	↓
• 5th: March	1998	0.7h	5.6h

Source: Customs and Tariff Bureau, MOF, Japan

Changes in the Time Required
(Air Cargo)

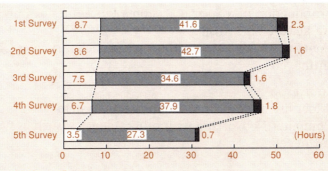

5th Survey Results:
Time for Customs Clearance reduced by 60% from the 4th Survey.

Source: Customs and Tariff Bureau, MOF, Japan

Changes in the Time Required
(Sea Cargo)

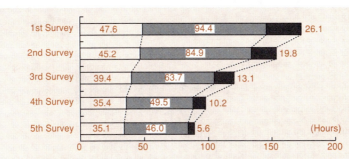

5th Survey Result:
Time for Customs Clearance reduced by 45% from the 4th Survey.

Source: Customs and Tariff Bureau, MOF, Japan

Reasons for reduction in Customs Clearance Time

Air Cargo:
1. Introduction of a Special Customs Procedure for Immediate Release on Arrival.
2. Computer Networking with other Agencies, such as Quarantine, etc.

Sea Cargo:
1. Wider use of Pre-Arrival Examination System.
2. Computer Networking with other Agencies, such as Quarantine, etc.

Source: Customs and Tariff Bureau, MOF, Japan

Trend of Usage of NACCS Systems
(Import by Sea/Air)

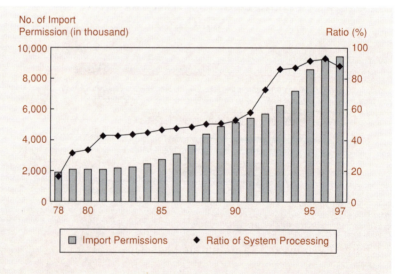

Source: Customs and Tariff Bureau, MOF, Japan

Effect of the Pre-Arrival Examination System
(Air Cargo)

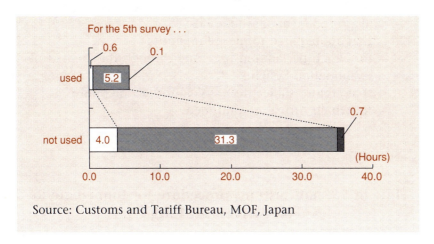

Source: Customs and Tariff Bureau, MOF, Japan

Effect of the Pre-Arrival Examination System
(Sea Cargo)

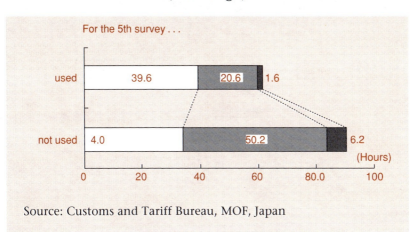

Source: Customs and Tariff Bureau, MOF, Japan

Special Customs Procedure for Immediate Release on Arrival (Air Cargo only)

- This procedure applies to goods:
  - that are required to release urgently;
  - for which declaration has gone through the Pre-Arrival Examination System;
  - that are not subject to physical inspection; and
  - for which Arrival is confirmed.

Source: Customs and Tariff Bureau, MOF, Japan

Flow of Special Customs procedure for Immediate Release on Arrival (Air Cargo only)

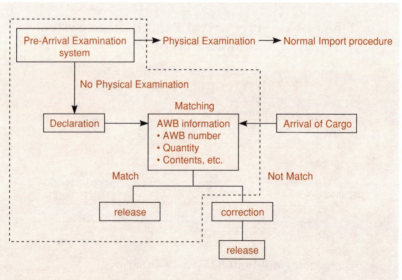

Source: Customs and Tariff Bureau, MOF, Japan

Annex IV
A Technical Assistance to Kingdom of Nepal for Efficiency Enhancement of Customs Operations: An Example of Asian Development Bank Assistance [1]

Introduction

Discussions of the Automated System for Customs Data (ASYCUDA) began in 1991 in Nepal. It is to be used as the core of the computerization program of the Department of Customs (DOC). It was proposed to be installed initially at the Tribhuvan International Airport, pending approval from United Nations Development Programme (UNDP). However, UNDP had subsequently advised that the budget for Nepal has been cut and priority was for rural development and livelihood projects. The government then requested the Bank to provide a grant for installing the system. A Fact-Finding Mission was fielded in April 1995 while the government committed to computerizing the DOC as required for implementing the system.

Background and Rationale

In June 1992, the Government embarked on a program of economic liberalization as embodied in Nepal's Eighth Five-Year Plan. They introduced new trade and industrial policies to open the economy to international trade and

---

[1] Taken from ADB, TA 2459, October 1995.

investment and to increase international competitiveness. Although there had been progress, the government still wants to improve government finances. Because customs collections are a major source of government revenue, they realized the need for improving the handling of transactions and remove impediments in its customs procedures.

The existing customs procedures, formalities, and documentation requirements are inefficient and complicated and are usually the cause of delay in the movement of goods. These inefficiencies contribute to the difficulties of foreign investments and ventures. The government also loses revenues and trade statistics are distorted because imported goods are often undervalued under the existing system. The lack of accurate and timely trade data hampers the progress of tariff administration and policy formulation.

The government has computerized clearance procedures and data processing as improvement of customs functions and procedures. The heart of the computerization system is the ASYCUDA, which was developed by the United Nations Conference for Trade and Development (UNCTAD). The system, which has several modules for different customs procedures, is aimed to provide a cost-effective solution to modernization of customs administration in developing countries. The government agreed to install ASYCUDA, rather than a tailor-made system which is more expensive. The system will be installed in phases, with the Bank-funded first phase limited to the Tribhuvan International Airport and DOC headquarters and will serve as the model for the applications at the border ports, and subsequent phases covering the dry ports at the India and Tibet borders. Depending on the success of the system's implementation under the Bank's technical assistance, the World Bank has proposed to integrate in its projects in Nepal the installation of ASYCUDA at Birgunj, the main border post to India.

Financial and economic benefits are expected to be very substantial. An indication of potential benefits in quantitative terms may be gauged from the experience of other countries using ASYCUDA.

The implementation of the recommendation for improving customs procedures and establishing a proper and transparent valuation system is one of the conditions for the second tranching of one of the Bank's projects.[2] The government has agreed to move toward a system in accordance with the Valuation Agreement of the World Trade Organization.

In light of the importance of reforms in the customs operations and administration and in support of the ongoing ISPL, it is desirable for the Bank to provide TA for implementing ASYCUDA and adopting a new valuation system based on the GATT Valuation Agreement. The proposed TA will promote the strengthening of the macroeconomic management in Nepal.

The Technical Assistance

The primary objective of the TA is to assist the Government in improving the efficiency and effectiveness of customs operations and increasing the yield of customs revenues, and to provide the government with better information needed to formulate and conduct economic and fiscal policies.

The TA has two components: automation of the data processing by installing ASYCUDA in the first phase, and capacity building of the DOC for a new system based on the Valuation Agreement. The first component includes configuring the ASYCUDA software package to the needs of DOC, and introducing rationalized and simplified customs procedures. Training of staff and other people involved on the new procedures will also be provided. The second component will focus on setting standard values for valuation and preparing a handbook of the procedures and guidelines for implementing the system. A training program on customs

---

[2] Loan No. 1229-NEP (SF): Industrial Sector Program Loan (ISPL).

valuation will be provided for customs officials and a publication on the procedures will be prepared and disseminated to concerned parties.

The TA is estimated to cost $1,454,000 equivalent. The Bank will provide $1,168,000 to cover the entire foreign exchange and part of the local currency cost of the TA. The government will bear the remaining cost of the TA, estimated at $286,000, of which a substantial amount will be used to refurbish the DOC offices.

The DOC will be the executing agency for the TA. The first component is expected to be completed in 18 months and the second one in 7 months. The TA is scheduled to complete in November 1997.

UNCTAD will be the consultant for the first component of the TA, as ASYCUDA is a proprietary software of the UNCTAD and can only be implemented by a team of experts from UNCTAD. All experts will perform their tasks in Kathmandu, except the international computer programmer who will be based in Switzerland, and the international electronic data processing expert, who will be based in Malaysia. Both will visit Kathmandu twice during the implementation. The second component will require a customs valuation expert, who will work with the UNCTAD experts.

The consultants will prepare an inception report, a draft final report, and a final report for each component. UNCTAD will submit a midterm report for the first component, and their final report will include an evaluation of the computerization program. The final report which will incorporate comments from the government and the Bank, will be submitted after the tripartite meeting on the draft final report.

All TA equipment financed by the Bank will be procured by the Bank with assistance from the Nepal Resident Mission.

The President's Recommendation

The President recommends that the Board approve the proposed technical assistance, on a grant basis, to His Majesty's Government of Nepal in an amount not exceeding the equivalent of $1,168,000 for the purpose of Efficiency Enhancement of Customs Operations.

Note on Contributors

Rafael Arana
Customs Attache' Permanent Representation of Spain
The European Union, Brussels

Hiroshi Arichi
Director
International Trade Organizations Division
Customs and Tariff Bureau
Ministry of Finance, Japan

Geoffrey Barrington
Industry Affairs Controller
British Airways, United Kingdom

Hans van Bodegraven
Director for Customs Policy and Legislation
Ministry of Finance, The Netherlands

James Goh
Chairman of the Board of Directors
Conference of Asia Pacific Express Carriers (CAPEC), Singapore

Patrick Heinesson
Head of Development Department
National Board of Customs, Sweden

Ibrahim bin Md. Isa
Senior Assistant Director of Customs
Royal Customs and Excise Department, Malaysia

Rob van Kuik
Senior Policy Adviser
Customs Policy and Legislation Directorate
Ministry of Finance, The Netherlands

Buenaventura Maniego
District Collector
Manila International Container Port
Bureau of Customs, Department of Finance, Philippines

Leo Nissinen
Deputy Director General
National Board of Customs, Finland

Robert Richardson
Manager
International Air Transport Association (IATA) Facilitation Services, Canada

Salvatore Schiavo-Campo
Senior Advisor on Governance and Public Management
Asian Development Bank